Art and the
built environment

=

A teacher's approach

LONGMAN GROUP LIMITED,
Longman House, Burnt Mill, Harlow, Essex CM20 2JE, England
and Associated Companies throughout the World.

First published 1982
Third impression 1984
ISBN 0 582 36195 8

Set in 10/12 point Baskerville
by HM Repros Phototypesetting Service,
Glasgow

Printed and bound in Great Britain by
William Clowes Limited, Beccles and London

Art and the built environment

A teacher's approach

Eileen Adams and Colin Ward

Published for the Schools Council by Longman

Acknowledgements

We are very conscious that in this book we are reporting, not our own work, but a collaborative effort, and we most gratefully acknowledge our collaborators. Firstly we are indebted to Ralph Jeffery HMI and to Ernest Goodman, formerly Headmaster of Manchester High School of Art and chairman of the Schools Council Art Committee, who were the instigators of this project, to Maurice Plaskow, Curriculum Officer at the Schools Council, who has consistently given us wise advice, to the members of the Art Committee, our sponsors, and to our own consultative committee, which has consisted of:

Keith Wheeler (Chairman)
Colin Lowson
Tony Francombe
Jeff Bishop
David Hall
John James
Mary Medd
Tessa Hope, followed by G D B Gray
and Valerie M Glauert
David Ollerenshaw, followed by Connie Passfield

We are also most grateful to the authors of trial materials developed for the project: Keith Wheeler of Leicester Polytechnic, Brian Goodey of Oxford Polytechnic, and Jeff Bishop of the School for Advanced Urban Studies, University of Bristol. We felt privileged to enrol these pioneers in relatively untried paths, so far as secondary education is concerned, in the service of this Project.

Our major indebtedness is of course to the schools and colleges involved in the work, both our trial institutions and associated schools, who were willing, without any obvious advantage to themselves, to welcome outsiders with a particular axe to grind. Many of the teachers, met almost by chance, have become firm friends, and many of the students and pupils, who took yet another guinea-pig assignment in their stride, have, if our assumptions are right, had an enhancing experience through their association with this Project. The schools and colleges to which we are particularly grateful are:

Banbury School, Oxon
Bridgewater Hall School, Milton Keynes
Edgebarrow School, Berkshire (for their Wapping and Rotherhithe project)
Gateway School, Leicester (for the first two years)
Hartcliffe School, Bristol
Kingsthorpe Upper School, Northampton
Lawrence Weston School, Bristol
Merrywood Girls School, Bristol
Parliament Hill School, London (for the first year of the Project)
Peter Symonds College, Winchester
Priory School, Portsmouth
Rotherham College of Arts and Community Studies
Sheredes School, Hoddesdon, Hertfordshire
Wakefield Urban Studies Centre (as a basis for the participation of several schools in the district, and of Wakefield College of Technology and Arts)
West Hatch High School, Chigwell, Essex
Ysgol Gyfun, Ystalyfera, West Glamorgan (which, apart from its own great contribution, served as a basis for the participation of several schools in South Wales: Cefn Hengoed School, Swansea, St Alban's School, Pontypool and Fairwater School, Cwmbran).

Grateful thanks, too, to those teachers who have allowed us to reproduce examples of their pupils' work – Tony Morgan, John Orton, John Morgan, Roger Standen, Derek Allport, John Akers, John James.

We are grateful to the Inner London Education Authority for the secondment of the Project Officer, to the staff of the Town and County Planning Association for tolerating a cuckoo in their nest, and to Rose Tanner for innumerable services.

Finally, the Project has profited greatly from the continual support and encouragement of several members of the Inspectorate, especially the late Daniel Shannon HMI, whose pioneering work in linking architects and planners with art teachers has been of immense benefit to us, and of many members of the Art Advisers' Association whose local support has been invaluable.

EILEEN ADAMS, Project Officer
COLIN WARD, Project Director

Art and the built environment

A Schools Council Project, based within the Education Unit of the Town and Country Planning Association 1976-80 and within the Design Education Unit at the Royal College of Art 1980-82.

The authors

Eileen Adams studied at Trent Park College, where she took a BEd degree in art and education, and later taught art at several London secondary schools. As Deputy Head of art at Pimlico School, she introduced the *Front Door* project before being seconded as Project Officer for the *Art and the Built Environment* Project. She is now a research fellow at the Royal College of Art working on a further phase of *Art and the Built Environment*.

Colin Ward worked in architecture for many years before training as a teacher at Garnett College. He was lecturer in charge of liberal studies at Wandsworth Technical College before becoming the TCPA's first Education Officer in 1971. He directed the *Art and the Built Environment* Project from 1976 to 1980. His books include *Streetwork: the Exploding School* (with Anthony Fyson); *British School Buildings: Designs and Appraisals*; *Vandalism*, and *The Child in the City*.

List of contributors

Many of the study methods used in the Project were originally devised by members of the consultative committee and others with experience of teaching about the built environment. In addition, Keith Gretton carried out a valuable evaluation which is summarized in an appendix but is also available in full from the Schools Council. Ken Baynes edited the book for publication.

Ken Baynes is Head of the Design Education Unit at the Royal College of Art. An author and designer, he was an instigator of the *Front Door* project at Pimlico School and is now co-director with Eileen Adams of the present phase of the *Art and the Built Environment* Project. His books include: *Attitudes in Design Education; About Design; Art in Society; Hospital Research and Briefing Problems,* and *The Art of the Engineer*.

Jeff Bishop is an architect who was drawn into environmental education through his work at the Architectural Psychology Research Unit at Kingston Polytechnic. Now a lecturer at the School for Advanced Urban Studies, University of Bristol, he is the author of the DES report *The Briefing Process in School Design,* and of *The Appraisal of Buildings: A Case Study and Critique of Approaches*.

Brian Goodey is Reader in Urban Design at Oxford Polytechnic. He is a consultant for the Council of Europe and has published widely on environmental perception, methods of urban interpretation and environmental education. His books include *Perception of the Environment; Images of Place,* and *Urban Walks and Town Trails*.

Keith Gretton trained as a mural painter and taught art for many years in secondary modern, grammar and comprehensive schools. He then taught painting at All Saints College, London, and has had 10 one-man exhibitions of paintings, prints and sculpture. He was until recently Head of the Art Department at Borough Road College, London, and is engaged on an examination of the teaching of architecture in secondary schools.

Keith Wheeler was Senior Lecturer in the School of Humanities, Leicester Polytechnic, and has been closely involved in the development of environmental education for the past 25 years. He is chairman of the Council for Environmental Education and is a member of the UNESCO/UNEP Environmental Education Programme. His many books include *Environmental Geography,* and *Insights Into Environmental Education*.

Introduction

The aim of this book

Since its inception in 1976, the *Art and the Built Environment* Project has grown steadily in scope and influence. Its most recent phase, which began in 1980, has seen the setting up of a nationwide network of curriculum development groups and extension of the age range to include the whole period of secondary education. Architects and planners have been joining teachers in planning and implementing a series of innovations in local schools. The long-term intention is to establish the study of the built environment as a normal part of the art curriculum in secondary schools.

The aim of this publication is to help that evolution. It sets out to make a contribution in four ways, corresponding to the parts into which the book is divided:

Part one: Art into townscape

Sets out the thinking behind the Project, describes the developments in education to which it relates and makes a case for the essential role of the art teacher in any study of the environment.

Part two: Study methods

Analyses the approaches to learning adopted by the Project, explains the reasoning behind each study method, gives a picture of the kind of results that might be expected and shows some examples of the work that was done.

Part three: Trial runs

Describes the direct involvement of teachers and students in the Project at A-level, in field studies, in general studies and in the 11–16 age range. It provides a realistic account of the impact of *Art and the Built Environment* work on a number of widely differing schools.

Part four: Conclusions

Sums up the Project team's experience so far and looks at the significance of those new developments that have already begun.

Taken together, these ingredients are intended to provide a practical handbook for art teachers. It will be possible to translate the Project's work directly into the studio or, more positively, into the study of the environment surrounding any school. The materials are readily available. Local buildings in towns and villages, including the school buildings themselves, must be the cheapest and most accessible of all educational resources. For *Art and the Built Environment* work they are the *only* essential ones.

However, experience has shown that great advantages can come from working with others. That is why the Project has now turned to the formation of local curriculum development groups. For members of these groups, the book should have a special usefulness. It can be made the basis for courses in which teachers, planners and architects join together to sample the Project's study methods or it can help to start discussions and give some form to curriculum experiments. These experiences can then be fed back into the Project to enrich and extend it and be made more widely available. This book is meant to be the start of a communication process not the end of it.

Because the nature of the Project has been to emphasize one neglected aspect of the art teacher's work, there has been a danger of appearing to recommend that existing courses should be scrapped. This is by no means the intention. The work recommended here is not an alternative to, or replacement of, what is already being done, but an important enlargement of it. In the future pattern of art and design education it should become a normal part of the work of the art teacher to complement his or her other well-established roles. Seen in that light, the Project and this book fall naturally into place as a part of the extraordinary growth in environmental concern which has marked the past decade. It shows how art teachers, as much as geographers or ecologists, have an absolutely central contribution to make to what is clearly going to be one of the great themes of the twentieth century.

Contents

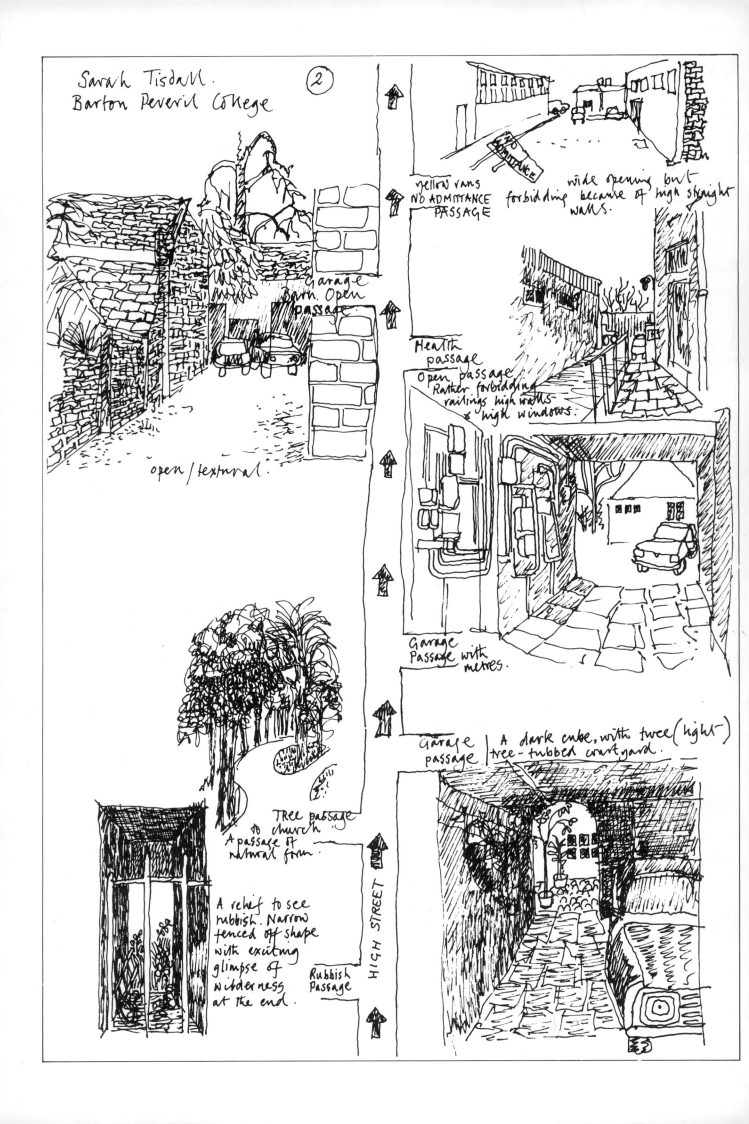

Sarah Tisdall.
Barton Peveril College

②

Garage dark open passage.

open/textural.

yellow vans
NO ADMITTANCE
PASSAGE

wide opening but forbidding because of high straight walls.

Health passage
Open passage
Rather forbidding
railings high walls
& high windows.

Garage
Passage with metres.

Garage passage

A dark cube, with tree (light) tree-tubbed courtyard.

Tree passage to church.
A passage of natural form.

A relief to see rubbish. Narrow fenced off shape with exciting glimpse of wilderness at the end.

Rubbish Passage

HIGH STREET

The Project

The original aims of the Project were:
a to enlarge the students' environmental perception and enable them to develop a 'feel' for the built environment,
b to enhance their capacity for discrimination and their competence in the visual appraisal of the built environment,
c to evolve generally applicable techniques and materials for achieving **a** and **b,**
d to disseminate these in a form suitable for teacher training and guidance.

To begin with this meant finding out how methods familiar in art education could be applied to a study of the environment. We found that this obliged art teachers to reconsider the purpose of observation, recording and analysis. For instance, they had to view art activities as a means of study rather than as a basis for picture making. The Project showed convincingly that art offers an appropriate framework for understanding the aesthetic and design aspects of the man-made world.

Art education, with its emphasis on direct experience and personal interpretation, encourages a feeling response which is basic to an understanding of the environment. What has become clear is that this kind of sensibility is learnt. Thus art education has an important role to play in developing awareness and discriminatory skills. Teachers involved in the Project have devised appropriate new study techniques to deal with this important aspect of art and environmental education. The critical aspects of the work were the most difficult because they were the least familiar and most threatening. However, it proved possible to introduce basic techniques for critical study which were effective.

The Project has not concentrated on the production of learning materials for pupils. Instead it has concerned itself with teachers' attitudes and how they think about their job. The conviction is that continuing support for the professional development of teachers is more important than the production of packs, kits and worksheets. The primary source material for *Art and the Built Environment* work is the environment itself. The Project has demonstrated that art teachers are best placed to devise the particular approaches for their own pupils. Materials for teacher training, including the present book, are intended as an introduction. The value of the Project's work lies principally in the model it offers for school-based curriculum development.

Although the research phase of the Project was based on a small number of trial schools where teachers worked individually, experience with a wider range of involvement during the development phase showed how effective cooperation between teachers could be. An important conclusion is that the establishment of curriculum development groups offers the encouragement and support necessary for their members to learn from collective experience. However, the effectiveness of the groups is strengthened when architects and planners join to work with teachers in promoting this area of study in schools.

In summary our recommendations are as follows:

1 *Art and the Built Environment* work is the concern of the art teacher.

2 It should be part of art, design and environmental education and can be incorporated into many existing syllabuses.

3 It is best promoted by support for the professional development of teachers and this can be done effectively through the establishment of working parties which will benefit from the inclusion of architects and planners.

Part One: Art into Townscape

feeling of room again
given by width of road and
amount of sky visible.
however, mass of traffic forms a
"alleyway" on right hand side of road.

LLOYDS BANK

ABBEY NATIONAL

BOO...

masses of
traffic.

MIKE GRIFFITHS

1 Aims and background of the Project

The *Art and the Built Environment* Project is an exploration of the role of art departments in environmental education in schools and further education colleges. The specific aims of the first phase of curriculum development were:

a to enlarge the students' environmental perception and enable them to develop a 'feel' for the built environment,
b to enhance their capacity for discrimination and their competence in the visual appraisal of the built environment,
c to evolve generally applicable techniques and materials for achieving these aims,
d to disseminate these in a form suitable for teacher training and guidance.

This book reports on the results and is itself intended as a major medium of dissemination.

From 1976 to 1980 the Project was based at the Town and Country Planning Association. Colin Ward, the Association's Education Officer, was its part-time Director. The Project Officer, serving full-time on secondment from the Inner London Education Authority, was Eileen Adams, previously Deputy Head of Art at Pimlico School, where she had for two years undertaken the *Front Door* Project which, because of its relevance to her subsequent work, is briefly described in Chapter 15.

The Project's age range

The brief confined the first phase of the project to the 16 – 19 age range. This reflected one of the main areas of educational concern at the time of its inception. The late 1970s saw the emergence of the new non-academic sixth-former and of the continuing debate, the end of which is not in sight, on resulting changes in the examination structure. We, in the Project team, have not regretted this confinement of our brief. It has helped, with so small a staff, to have limited ends and, in practice, it has not limited the impact of the work to the upper end of the school. If you believe that the sixth form tail wags the secondary school dog, then you may assume that the teacher who undertakes art-based environmental work with sixth-formers will be bound to develop similar work further down the school. This has certainly been our experience and we feel justified in reporting on relevant work below the age range where that resulted from the project's influence. The most recent phase of the Project has, in any case, seen the extension of the age range to cover the whole period of secondary education.

The 16 – 19 age range in educational institutions is a very heterogeneous group. It includes the 'traditional' sixth-formers preparing for an A-level in Art, and students preparing for O-levels and even CSE. In addition there are their classmates doing art as a non-examination option, the 'new' sixth-formers and a variety of further education students in both examination and non-examination courses. In two of our trial institutions there were students on a very interesting and unusual course called General Education Through Art and Design (GEAD), promoted by the Yorkshire and Humberside Committee for Further Education.

When the Project began we had hoped to explore the potentiality of the kind of work we are recommending for students who were combining an Art or Design A-level with, for example, one of the geography exams which has a requirement of urban fieldwork, or for students who were sitting also for one of the three A-levels in environmental studies, or for the Oxford A-level in Design. In practice, although we have encountered such students, the nature of sixth form work, in which each student is often working to an individual programme, is such that it has proved to be impossible to generalize about the cross-currents between subjects.

The TCPA background

The Project was entrusted, not to a college or department of education, but to the Town and Country Planning Association, which is a voluntary organisation, essentially an environmental pressure group. The TCPA was founded in 1899 by the garden city pioneer Ebenezer Howard and his original disciples to propagate the decentralist ideas that led to the government policy of new towns and expanded towns after the second world war. Its activities have expanded since then into advocacy of regional planning, the involvement of the general public in the process of planning, and the provision of 'planning aid' by analogy with legal aid.

In the late 1960s the widespread public dissatisfaction with the results of planning policy on British towns and cities led to the demand for 'public participation in planning'. The government appointed a committee, chaired by the late Arthur Skeffington, to consider how participation might be made effective. Its report, *People and Planning,* among many other things recommended that education about town planning should be 'part of the way in which all secondary schools make children conscious of their future civic duties', that it should be 'part of the liberal and civic studies within places of further education', and that the training of teachers should include 'a similar emphasis on civic studies, including the philosophy of town and country planning.'[1]

To teachers, this sounds suspiciously like the 'jug' theory of education — treating the child as a jug into which wisdom about whatever is currently conceived as a social issue should be poured: road safety, contraception, race relations, and so on. Nevertheless, the Skeffington Report provided a valuable incentive for the TCPA to set up its education unit. In 1971, Colin Ward (with a background of architecture followed by teaching) and Anthony Fyson (with a background of town-planning followed by teaching) were appointed to initiate the unit.

The emphasis of their work was on the urban environment, simply because there already existed a well-established tradition of rural studies and many existing bodies concerned with it. It was their conviction that the

TCPA's role should be the encouragement of education for mastery of the environment, seeking a situation where the skills to manipulate the environment are accessible to all the people and not merely to an articulate minority. They asked: 'if the aim of environmental education is not to make children the masters of their environment, what else can it be for?' This attitude carried over into *Art and the Built Environment* and helped to determine many of its approaches.

They thus found themselves in the same camp as another educational pressure group, the Politics Association, whose mentor, Bernard Crick, declares that 'Civic education must be aimed at creating citizens. If we want a passive population, leave well alone.' The TCPA education unit consequently advocated an 'issue-based' or 'problem-oriented' approach to the environment and developed a range of techniques, methods and facilities for active environmental learning. These included gaming, simulations and role-play, didactic theatre, town trails (devised *by* as well as *for* the class), and urban studies centres (by analogy with the field centres which have had such a valuable effect on education about the rural environment). Anthony Fyson coined the word *streetwork*[2], to avoid the term 'urban fieldwork', as a description for the range of approaches to the study of the built environment in the street, rather than in the classroom, which we also advocate in the Project.

Most important of all, the TCPA education unit established a medium of communication with teachers in its journal BEE, the *Bulletin of Environmental Education*.

The Project's method

The Schools Council inherited from the pioneering curriculum development projects (funded by the Nuffield Foundation) a method consisting in essence of the devising of teaching materials by the Project staff in consultation with experienced practitioners, their 'validation' through use in trial schools, and their subsequent publication for general adoption. The development of the materials was normally accompanied by conferences and courses in their use for teachers. In some cases, the most obviously successful example being the *Geography for the Young School Leaver* Project, a network of local groups of teachers has been set up, both to supplement the materials through locally developed teaching aids, and in order to bring into the scope of the project's influence, teachers and schools who have not had direct contact with the project staff.

It is evident that in those areas of the curriculum where there is a clearly defined body of knowledge to be communicated, the production of teaching materials can be particularly successful. However, with that minority of Schools Council projects concerned with the arts subjects, it has not usually been found that this kind of strategy is the most suitable one. Some have resolutely declined to produce classroom materials for their subjects, conscious that this is not the way in which such teachers work.

Few art teachers hand out books at the beginning of a period and encourage the class to work through a specific activity. However, it is clear that books and other published materials influence art teaching. For example, there are two series of books, in versions for both teachers and pupils, produced by Kurt Rowlands, which have evidently affected the way in which teachers work. But we have never seen these books in use in the classroom. This suggests that, so great is the premium upon originality or spontaneity in the art teaching world that few who use his methods are willing to acknowledge his influence. More than one teacher has said to us, with satisfaction, 'the Art Room is the one place in the school, apart from the Gym, which is not dominated by books.'

We appreciate these reservations. On the other hand, it was hard to see how our Project could be influential without some form of publication. Since our terms of reference included such aims as the enhancement of students' capacity for discrimination and their competence in environmental appraisal, we decided that it was highly desirable to issue a series of manuals of environmental *exercises* designed to achieve these results. By comparison with other curriculum development projects we have been most fortunate in one important respect: the high costs of publishing such materials were offset by the availability of BEE which became the medium through which our approaches could be disseminated quickly. This meant that we could publish as we went along and get valuable information back from an experienced audience beyond our trial schools.

We were aware that there were several hazards in publishing these materials. Some art teachers would find them too prescriptive, some might feel them alien to the general outlook of art education and would assume, on the evidence of these materials, that the Project had nothing to offer them. Some on the other hand might actually be inhibited from developing approaches of their own, assuming that there was something sacrosanct about the study methods advocated. Most users, however, cheerfully selected and rejected from the range of approaches offered, and adapted them to their own needs in developing techniques of their own. We assume that exactly the same will happen with the approaches to study presented here.

At the same time, it has become obvious in running courses for teachers in connection with the Project, that when they themselves have tried out the activities recommended for their students, they have discovered that something valuable for their own teaching emerged. Some who were hostile to the techniques we propagated were won over to them simply by undertaking them. This does not 'validate' the approaches: we simply conclude that *involvement* in any activity changes one's view of it. Again this is something which we assume will happen with this book.

The final piece in the jigsaw has been to begin the creation of a network of local curriculum development groups to carry the work of the Project forward. In 1980, Eileen Adams joined the Design Education Unit at the Royal College of Art to bring this about. By January 1981 at least 20 groups were in existence and 15 more were planned. When Schools Council funding has ended in August 1982, *Art and the Built Environment* should have become a self-perpetuating activity involving students and teachers in working with architects and planners and with the direct support of local education authorities and the design professions.

tall/narrow/enclosed
very vertical emphasis
cars large to space

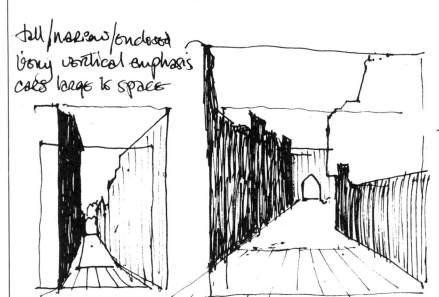

focal point archway.
Roadway most evident

limited vision. emphasis changes to areas
within gaps. building = dark + light shapes -

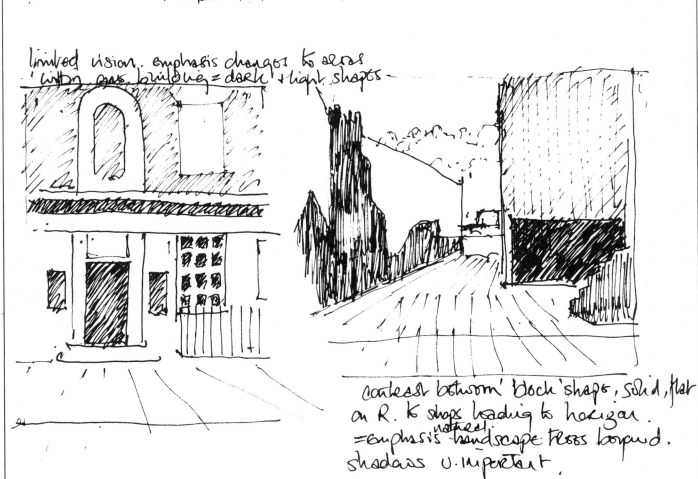

contrast between 'block' shape, solid, flat
on R. to shops leading to horizon.
= emphasis natural landscape trees beyond.
shadows v. important.

impossible to ignore cars
& people even when concentrating
on large forms.

2 Six things that the Project is not

During their work on the Project, the team found that there were a series of characteristic misconceptions which came up time and time again. This chapter is an attempt to deal with them from the outset.

1 It is not a take-over bid for the art department

Over the years art teachers have felt continually obliged to assert the autonomy of their subject. Art is an autonomous, self-justifying activity. Our experience in talking to art teachers all over the country is that whatever the virtues of the movement towards design departments, art teachers have seen them as restrictive rather than supportive. Consequently, when this Project has sought to involve them in environmental education they have quite often seen our efforts as yet another constraint on the autonomy of art as a school activity. Not only this, but we have felt obliged continually to reassure art teachers that our own propagation of an environmental approach does not imply that we think this should be the whole work of the art department, in the sixth form or anywhere else in the school.

> **Our attitude is that art is a mode of perception and that the understanding and appraisal of the environment in emotional, subjective and sensory yet qualitative terms is quite naturally one aspect of the aims of art in education, just as it is quite naturally one aspect of environmental education as a whole.**

2 It is not a course in topographical draughtsmanship

The first response to the idea of this Project is to think of works of art which happen to have the built environment as their subject. This is the most obvious interpretation and it is perfectly true that in schools and colleges associated with the Project some superlative drawings and paintings have been produced, whose subject has been streets and buildings, rather than those interesting objects scattered around the art room or derived from the students' imaginations. It cannot be said that these works do *not* enhance the environmental understanding of the people who made them. Many people would say that the simple act of recording a place adds to our comprehension of it. Quite outside the art world, this claim has been made for the use of field sketching as a geographical technique. We think these claims are justified. Nevertheless, to put an exclusive importance on the topographical accuracy of a drawing or painting of the urban scene is to ask that a work of art should be so valued according to how well it conveyed the disposition, weight, solidity, and construction of a building or

assemblage of buildings. Does the eye deduce the layout or site plan from the view presented? Is the perspective correct? However important these factors are in our context, few artists, art critics or art educators would accept that they are the exclusive criteria for evaluating a work of art.

Art in schools is *product-oriented*. The pupil or student produces a work of art and this is assessed. In an examination class it becomes a testimony to the level of excellence achieved. It is displayed in an exhibition which proves to children, parents and teachers that the art department is doing its job and doing it well. Part of the reluctance of some teachers to undertake the kind of work recommended by the *Art and the Built Environment* Project is that it may not result in such a work of art. Ralph Jeffery of the Art Inspectorate was faced with the same difficulty — the fact that teachers are in the habit of seeing the environment merely as a quarry for looting materials to be worked up back in the art room. He took the unusual step in a course he ran for teachers at Chichester, of relieving them of pens, pencils, felt-tips, cameras and note-books, so that they would be obliged to experience the streets of the city, without any means of recording the experience. No teacher connected with the Project has, to our knowledge, taken so drastic a step. Some have even taken the view that the kind of annotated drawing we recommend as a means of critical appraisal is 'a good drawing spoilt by all that writing'.

> **To the objection that art is by definition a creative activity, and that consequently environmental activity must be legitimised by resulting in a work of art, our response is that perception itself is a creative act. The Project is about experiencing and understanding the qualities of the built environment through art activity, not essentially about making works of art.**

3 It is not propaganda for 'good taste'

'What do we do with the fifth year leavers?', asked John Eggleston, Director of the Schools Council *Design and Craft Education* Project. 'All too often we devise a course called Design for Living, which culminates in a trip down to the Design Centre in London, to show them what they ought to like.' We too have frequently met the assumption that our task is to teach children what they ought to like, but we are fortunate that the period of our Project coincides with a period of soul-searching by architects and planners. They are themselves rejecting the more ephemeral tenets of the modern movement in architecture and design. In the 1930s and 1940s, Design Education often meant bringing into the classroom a collection of teapots and attempting to persuade the class that this product of the Staffordshire trade was bad (all that meaningless machine-made decoration), that this teapot shaped like a thatched cottage, with the roof coming off as a lid and the chimney as the knob on top, was intrinsically bad and dishonest, while this third teapot was an OK Bauhaus-designed functional sphere, with few necessary excrescences. That same teacher, now retired, has of course long since abandoned the Bauhaus tea-pot (its virginal white surface disfigured by tannin-stains and chips) and has on the shelf such an amusing and valuable collection of tea-pots designed to look like something else.

Designers themselves have followed the public in rejecting the functionalist ornament-equals-pornography approach to design, in favour of an approach which is humbler, more tentative, more eclectic and more subtle. An identical approach is implied by the Project's insistence that all environments can be studied and that all have something to offer environmental experience.

4 It is not propaganda for the broken-down picturesque

The great architectural teacher W R Lethaby remarked ruefully that the English are in love with the broken-down picturesque, and certainly John Piper confesses to an attachment to what he calls 'pleasing decay'. Constable too, declared that '. . . old rotten planks, slimy posts and brickwork — I love such things. As long as I do paint, I shall never cease to paint such places . . .' Perhaps it is in observing and lovingly recording these aspects of the environment that the approach of the art department is likely to be most distinct from that of other subjects in the school curriculum involved in environmental education. This is certainly observable in the work of our trial institutions. We have seen paintings based on atmospheric pollution that make no moral judgement — merely a beautiful pattern. Broken windows with their irregular mosaic of light and darkness frequently recur, unaccompanied by comments on the evils of neglect and vandalism.

Where are the calls for environmental action? Aren't we encouraging self-indulgent sentimental decadence, when we should be aiming to rear a generation of environmental crusaders? This is a very old and recurrent issue, in life as well as in education, and from Plato to the current orthodoxy in Russia and China there has always been the demand that art should serve a moral purpose which is socially approved.

The first comment that has to be made is that while art can be very powerful as social comment and as propaganda, we have to defend the integrity and autonomy of the artist, and the right to make a statement which is not part of the Social Problems Industry. This is the schoolchild's right as much as it is David Hockney's. The second response is the observation that squalor is in the eye of the beholder. 'I never saw an ugly thing in all my life', cried William Blake, and the same point comes from Ancel Morgan, head of art at the Wilson Marriage School, Colchester, commenting to us on the work of his pupils. 'They can't do anything horrible', he said. The environmental improver may deprecate the peeling paint on battered doors, but to the artist, the surface it reveals is fascinating for the patina of time and change and natural forces on the artefacts of men. The exposed party wall of a demolished house may cry out for attention from the Civic Trust, but the artist, and perhaps particularly the young artist, will see in the flapping wallpaper and faded distemper an evocation of the generations who lived there, even of their assumptions about interior decoration, just as

the naturalist will note that the raspberries in the unkempt garden are of a variety not marketed for 30 years, and will be sorry to see the improving effect of municipal crazy paving and flowering cherries in the General Improvement Area.

There *is* genuine conflict, an aesthetic conflict here, and we should not pretend that it does not exist. If our students prefer as subjects the haphazard accumulation of the detritus of the past, rather than the architecture of our own day isn't it just because of the boorish crudity of many of the examples of contemporary architecture that they actually encounter in their daily lives: the run-of-the-mill, system-built school building and the unloved council estate which surrounds it?

The ideological collapse of the modern movement in architecture, and the swing against 'comprehensive redevelopment' in planning and housing, both imply that our students may be right in their preference for environments which exhibit time and change and the accidents of history. We could probably claim with justification that if the people who created the typical local environment of the late twentieth century had in their youth lovingly delineated the pathetic remnants of other people's past environments, they would have been less ready in adulthood to deny the importance of history, sentiment and all those emotions which tie a person to a place.

The aim of the Project, however, has not been to encourage students to make art works of picturesque and evocative ruins. It has been to make them aware of conflicts where they exist and to urge them to cultivate the habit of making judgements.

5 It is not an environmental improvement scheme

An environmental activity carried out by schools which was once very rare and is now much more frequently encountered, is the design and execution of a mural, a sculptural or decorative scheme in the local environment. It might be the painting of a gable end, or of the walls of an underpass, or it might be the incorporation of ceramic objects made in school in the external walls of a new building in the locality. These are highly desirable activities: they symbolize the recognition that the young have a part to play in the reshaping of the habitat, or they exemplify the faith that vandalism would be less endemic if young people had a chance to make a legitimate imprint on their surroundings.

If this kind of activity is praiseworthy in the outside environment, we believe that it should be taken for granted in the school itself. Quite obviously the decoration of the school should be the work of the pupils. This is by no means a generally accepted principle. One very well-known teacher of design was anxious that a much needed additional building on the campus of his school should be considered as a design and construction exercise for the pupils themselves: the kind of opportunity that only happens once in a generation. The story he told us of the obstacles that were put in the way of achieving this is a sobering tale. One by one, these obstacles — the opposition of the county architects' department which was responsible for the premises, of the local planning authority and the administrators of the building regulations — were overcome, and the building actually got built.

Sometimes, of course, the quality of environmental improvements undertaken by schools leaves much to be desired. We have seen more than one example of the transformation of a patch of waste land into an 'environmental amenity', winning national awards for the school concerned, which has consisted of a badly designed seat surrounded by fussy paving and inappropriate planting. Such examples in no way invalidate the principle, particularly if, as educators, we believe that the process is more important than the product. If anything, they point to the need for the kind of sophisticated environmental awareness which we would like to develop in and out of school. We applaud the idea of the involvement of school-children in environmental improvements.

They are, however, beyond the scope of this stage of the *Art and the Built Environment* Project which has concentrated on response, analysis and appraisal in connection with the existing and directly experienced environment.

6 It is not sociology, politics or economics

Very often, when we have explained the aims and approaches of this Project to teachers, including art teachers, they have responded with the suggestion, put as kindly as possible, that there is something dreadfully superficial about an approach to the environment which isolates the visual, sensory, and subjective aspects, to the exclusion of the social and political or economic realities which are the true determinants of the character of our surroundings. Often, when we describe the project to architects and town planners, the same objection arises. Our reply is not to deny the importance of these other factors (and indeed the whole thrust of the TCPA's educational activities has been to stress them) but to assert that in that small section of the school student's time-table which is labelled 'art', visual and aesthetic values should be uppermost. It amazes us that art teachers should think otherwise.

We can perfectly well conceive of an integrated approach to the environment where each discipline complemented the others in developing the students' environmental awareness, but it was totally beyond the power and influence of a curriculum development project on this scale to achieve this kind of integration (just as it has been beyond the power of the course planners in the universities, polytechnics and other teacher-training establishments, where departmental barriers are as strong as they always were).

We have tended to throw the question back at the objectors, because in our view the environmental horrors of so much post-war redevelopment have been the result, not so much of the economic and political determinants, but of the exclusion from consideration of visual, sensory, symbolic and aesthetic values. This is nowhere better illustrated than in the field of local authority housing — the homes of a third of the population. Anyone in the housing industry in a city, small town or new town, will confirm that there is an order of preference among present or potential tenants, among the houses and flats they have commissioned. Those which are most popular, whether in Manchester or Milton Keynes, Runcorn or Rotherham, are those which conform most closely to ordinary people's visual perception of house and home. The highest praise that a local authority tenant can give to his home is that 'it doesn't look like a council house'.

What might have saved our rulers and their professional advisers would have been a greater and more sensitive attention to 'the intelligence of feeling' — that whole area of human experience which is the subject of this Project.

SWING WINDOWS

LAID BACK FROM OTHERS
(VERY DULL)

FAVOURITE
(ORNAMENTAL)

STONE + FLINT

RED TILES

SAME STYLE

CONCRETE SLABS

MODERN DESIGN
(EYE CATCHING)

CLOSE PACKED STONES

SLIDING WINDOWS

ORDINARY BRICKS

3 Getting environmental education into focus

> The city as we know it, the soft city of illusion, myth and nightmare is as real, maybe more real than the hard city one can locate on maps, in statistics, in monographs on urban sociology and architecture.
>
> JONATHAN RABAN, *Soft City*

Under various subject headings, a field of school activity which has grown steadily throughout the 1970s is environmental education. The phrase itself is equivocal. It can imply, for example, the *use* of the environment — instead of the classroom — as an educative milieu for a variety of school subjects. It can imply education *about* the environment, treated as a classroom topic like any other. Or it can imply the direct use of the environment as a means to the understanding, appreciation and conservation of the environment.

At the beginning of the decade, a widely accepted definition (the 'Nevada Declaration') was that:

'environmental education is the process of recognizing values and clarifying concepts in order to develop the skills and attitudes necessary to understand and appreciate the interrelatedness among man, his culture and his biophysical surroundings. Environmental education also entails practice in decision-making, and self-formulation of a code of behaviour about issues concerning environmental quality.'[1]

At that time, for most people, including most teachers, environmental education was interpreted as education about the *natural* environment, which is 'good', and the threat to it from the built environment, which is 'bad'. Or it was considered to be concerned exclusively with the conservation of natural resources, the crisis of energy consumption, or with pollution and its effect on the habitat. Much less frequently was environmental education considered to be concerned with the towns and cities where most of this country's children live and attend school. All through the decade, British teachers addressing conferences on the subject organized by bodies like UNESCO or the Council of Europe found that their colleagues in other countries were surprised that the built environment should be considered a major theme of environmental education. This is by no means to suggest that British schools as a whole are more advanced in this area of their work than those of other countries. In our experience it is very often the enthusiasm, the tenacity and understanding of an individual teacher that is significant, rather than any provision in the official curriculum of the school.

Nevertheless, there was a steady growth in the 1970s of 'environmental studies' as an examinable subject in the secondary schools, a growing emphasis on 'environmental' geography and on environmental aspects of history, English, social and community studies. When Douglas MacGregor, of the then Chorley College of Education,

made a survey among teachers to see who was involved in environmental education he found that it was claimed to be the concern of every conceivable subject from RE to modern dance.[2] The claims made were not fanciful. The dance teacher, for example, declared that this activity was concerned with the spatial and sensory exploration of the environment: it developed spatial awareness.

Similarly, when Peter Berry conducted a survey of 400 secondary schools for the Conservation Society, asking, among other things, which departments were involved in environmental education, the answers came to geography 73%, biology 59%, science 52%, general studies 37% and history 33%, moving down to a small percentage of 'other departments' which included also-rans, home economics, English and art.[3] Admittedly this was a rough-and-ready survey, but it indicated, as many advisers and inspectors readily corroborate, that in the growing emphasis on environmental education, the arts subjects, and art itself, have played a very small part. The affective relationship between our pupils and the environment, the area of sentiments and feelings about the environment, is neglected.

This is precisely the field of concern of the Project. In traditional modes of environmental enquiry the urge to quantify and classify has been strong, but in the context of this Project we are more concerned with a qualitative analysis, the making of judgements concerned with aesthetic experience and emotional response. The work is at the interface of art, design and environmental education. Although all these areas have interests and concerns elsewhere, they each have a unique and special contribution to make to an understanding of the shaping of our surroundings.

Any systematic approach to environmental education requires interdisciplinary study. We undertake a descriptive and evaluative analysis of the environment in order to make sense of it. Subject disciplines may be considered merely as languages: ways of knowing. Each discipline, with its own concepts and ways of understanding offers specialist approaches to study. In different contexts one may be more appropriate than another, or perhaps we cannot have a really complete picture of anything until we have approached it from different viewpoints.

The environment as a theme is certainly an example of this. One type of study is no *better* than another, for they each give only a partial understanding. No subject discipline can offer a comprehensive understanding of the environment. However, various study approaches may be seen as complementary. There is a wide range of interpretations and possibilities that schools have not chosen to exploit, particularly in connection with ideas about our shaping of future environments.

In schools the tendency has been to promote environmental study as an objective, scientific, geographical, historical or sociological study. Children are rarely asked to draw conclusions or make judgements on the basis of their own experience of the environment. They are seen merely as collectors or recorders of information, and rarely as sources, interpreters or critics. The environment is thus seen in the context of academic study, involving only measurement and quantification. This was apparent in a number of our trial schools, where sixth-formers found it difficult to conceive of an urban study in terms other than those of questionnaires, surveys and mapping.

Yet the ways in which each of us interprets the environment are much more complex. David Wisdom, one of the architects involved in *Front Door* work at Pimlico School, a forerunner of the present study, observes that:

'We can perceive the environment in a number of ways: as a static reality — a coal hole cover, a cat on a fence; as a dynamic reality — a series of systems, finance, transport; a changing reality — it used to be like this, and could be . . .
These can be studied through established disciplines — the static reality through art; the dynamic reality through urban geography and economics; the changing reality through history and social studies.'

The academic basis of the school curriculum, where subject disciplines create parallel lines of study, completely ignores the complex interrelationships between them, which are hardly ever examined. Although individual subjects offer useful means of analysis of various aspects of environmental experience, there needs to be greater attention to the synthesis of that experience, and to the child's developing ability to understand and explain that experience.

Attitudes and values

Environmental education should not only involve a knowledge of the physical world, but should be concerned with how people feel about their environment, how they relate to it, how they are affected by it and how they affect it. Pioneers of this area of the curriculum in Britain like George Martin and Keith Wheeler have always insisted on this. It implies, they declare:

'a progressive development of a sense of concern for the environment based on a full and sensitive understanding of the relationship of man to his surroundings . . . it provides rich educational opportunities to think, compare, analyse, synthesize and research.'[4]

Their view is upheld by the Inspectorate:

'UNESCO has stated that one of the goals of environmental education is "to provide every person with the opportunities to acquire the knowledge, values, attitudes, commitment and skills needed to protect and improve the environment." By the age of 16, pupils might reasonably be expected to view their surroundings with eye both appreciative and critical; show developing attitudes of concern towards their environment and the environment of others; in so far as environmental issues are concerned, have a basis on which to develop the ability to make informed decisions affecting themselves and society — and the interest to do so.'

The Project suggests that environmental education is also about the attitudes and values we develop individually and personally through our interaction with the environment. Our long term aim is that people should be better prepared to play a more creative and participatory role in shaping their environment. But participation demands higher levels of awareness, interest, concern for and understanding of the environment. It obliges us to think critically about it.

Experience, judgement

What messages are pupils receiving from the typical current environmental education programmes? Dominated by objective, scientific, historical, sociological and statistical approaches to study, for many pupils environmental education is pollution, shopping surveys and traffic counts, the collection of facts and figures. You've got to look it up in the local authority's structure plan (for the present), *Kelly's Directory* (for the past), plot it on a graph or check it in a table of statistics for it to be acceptable. The validity of direct experience or personal values is negated, except perhaps in the approach of the English class. There is much investigation and recording of information, but little interpretation or critical appraisal.

No teacher in the world of environmental education would dream of denying that we need to encourage active learning in which children not only record, but explain and evaluate their experience of the environment. This point has arisen time and again in our own work with sixth-formers, where students unused to experiential learning and to the demands of critical study have found it difficult to make sense of their own experience, to form judgements or to express opinions.

Children learn through experience — but through experience of what? Often it is second–hand experience through books or classroom reconstructions of what the teacher thinks they ought to know. They are not encouraged to be educationally responsible. They should be learning through their own direct experience of life, and should be encouraged to take direct responsibility for their own education.

These truisms of teacher training have come to life for us in the course of our work. For example, there were certain schools in our project which adhered to a concept of the 'core curriculum' which included notions of direct exposure to environmental stimuli and to a personal response to this. These schools took the work in their stride. Similarly, the environmental exercises in later chapters of this book have been seized upon by teachers in higher education who declare that their first year degree students have been so confined by academic A-level teaching in their final years at school, that they have never had the opportunity to undertake the kind of work this Project recommends. They have used these exercises in order to open up their students' perception and imagination to the responsibility of reacting individually to their surroundings.

Design education

Bruce Archer describes design as:

'that area of human experience, skills and knowledge that reflects man's concern with the appreciation and adaptation of his surroundings in the light of his material and spiritual needs. In particular it relates with configuration, composition, meaning, value and purpose in man-made phenomena.'[5]

Our own experience is that teachers involved in design education tend to take a rather narrower view, and that design education in many schools continues to emphasize graphic and product design, the making of artefacts, and that the environment is merely seen as the sum total of these. The view that regards design as a hotchpotch of the 'practical' subjects concerned with 'making things' reinforces this impression, and does not make adequate provision for environmental design or systems design, which do not have a similar outcome.

The same criticism is made within the design education world. Peter Green, for example, suggests that:

'materials for design education concentrate on skills and techniques without engaging teachers in the basic design issues. The tendency is still towards a rather superficial approach with the emphasis on style, skills and appearances. There is little thought-provoking material about why things are designed and produced and whether they meet our needs.'[6]

It is in these areas of design education, which tend to be neglected in practice, that the work of the Project could be helpful. The work is firmly based in sensory experience and visual/tactile modes of study. We are concerned with how people *feel* about their surroundings — a theme which is at the heart of the development of design awareness.

We should recognize and promote — rather than pay lip service to — the separate and distinct contributions of a range of subject disciplines in the field of design education — not only art, craft and home economics, but also, in the context of environmental design, social studies, economics, geography, history and English. Design education is concerned with thinking and feeling as well as with making and doing. As the policy statement of the National Association for Design Education declares, 'design is concerned with the making of the environment and the relations and behaviour of the people within the environment. It is as much concerned with non-material aspirations as with the physical.'[7]

The missing component in environmental education

The words 'environmental education' are a portmanteau or hold-all for a great variety of interests and school activities, but there is a remarkable unanimity as to which aspects are most neglected. In 1978 a final report was issued by the Working Party on Environmental Education convened by the Environmental Board of the DOE. For this working party Professor Peter Hall and Sally Burningham interviewed over 60 people, active in all areas of environmental education. They reported that:

'Urban environmental education was seen as having a number of vital components, some of which are almost totally missing from our present system. The aesthetic and emotional responses formed one of the most important and neglected areas. Our total lack of attention to visual education, to teaching people to *see* was reiterated time and again by those interviewed; they found this one of the most worrying features of our education system and one that had had disastrous consequences. The fostering of a sense of place and an awareness of roots was seen as particularly vital today when so much experience is second-hand . . .'[8]

4 Art education and the environment

It should by now be clear to all thoughtful educationists that the long domination of English education by cognitive based studies pursued through verbal and numerical modes needs to be reduced, and the educational diet of our young people needs to be more adequately balanced by a far greater concern for their feelings, intuition and expressive needs, expressed through visual images. Art can be seen to have the potential to redress the imbalance prevailing since it is deeply and constantly concerned with 'non-linear' response and understanding, with the intuitive 'leap' and with the whole field of visual imagery.

ERNEST GOODMAN

The Project does not subscribe to a single unifying theory of art education, but has found a number of current interpretations useful. They identify and describe the possible roles of the art teacher in general education and help to define them more clearly. In this chapter we attempt to present these in a coherent pattern and show how they relate to environmental education in general and the Project in particular.

Earlier Schools Council projects concerned with art education have indicated the range and bias of existing practice. Art as expression still seems to be the dominant theme. Our impression is that the bias of many art teachers towards production skills, and their relative neglect of perceptual, conceptual and critical skills, serve to inhibit the development of art-based environmental work. The *Art and the Built Environment* Project encourages art teachers to reconsider the range of their responsibilities. It invites them to encompass areas other than the expressive domain, which seems to have been promoted at the expense of other important areas of development in the student's range of experience.

The Project has been concerned with the particular role of the art teacher in environmental education. Its aims, concerned with encouraging a subjective response and the development of critical skills, are, in our view, also central to the aims of art education. We stress sensory experience, emotional response and discriminatory skills. All these are elements which recent interpretations identify with art in schools. Similarly, viewed from the point of view of environmental education, art can permit ways of learning and perceiving which are a necessary and vital complement to the objective, academic and scientific study of towns. There is no other subject in schools which can contribute so much to the development of critical thinking in relation to townscape.

One particularly helpful way of clarifying this interrelationship between a holistic view of art education and a holistic view of environmental education is to use Brian Allison's suggested division of art education into four domains. He identifies the expressive domain; the perceptual domain; the analytical/critical domain; and the historical/cultural domain. He declares that:

'to be educated in art . . . means to be perceptually developed and visually discriminative, to be able to realise the relationships of materials to the form and function of art expression and communication, to be able to critically analyse and appraise art forms and phenomena, and to be able to realise the historical context of what is encountered and to be able to appreciate the contributions to and functions within, differing cultures and societies that art makes.'[1]

His view is that it is the concept of the practising artist as examplar for art education that has unnecessarily emphasized the importance of the expressive domain. This makes sense in the context of *Art and the Built Environment*. The demands of the Project have stressed the analytical/critical domain, but in fact the work relates to all four areas. The communication of an enlarged subjective, affective response to townscape is based in the perceptual and expressive domains, the development of discriminatory and critical skills in the analytical/critical domain and the full comprehension of the meaning of townscape, in the historical/cultural domain.

It is worth looking at each of these areas in turn.

The analytical/critical domain

A helpful argument for a reconsideration of the art teacher's role in relation to the development of discriminatory and critical skills may be found in the paper on Art Education included in the series of discussion papers *Curriculum 11–16* produced by the Inspectorate. This explains that while people make judgements all the time within the limits of their personal experience and ability, it is not a fixed capacity. It can be modified and improved. The teacher can intervene to extend and develop the students' critical capabilities. A few quotations from the paper will illustrate its insistence on this point[2]:

'. . . the essence of the contribution which art makes here lies in judgement and decision . . .'

'. . . the forming and informing of these judgements by practice and enrichment is a principal aim of art in schools.'

'. . . the principal skills developed by the practice of art lie in the ability to communicate visually and the power of discrimination — the recognition that as the Newsom Report put it, "Pupils are people who have a capacity to form a right judgement".'

Brian Allison's view is that many art teachers are still predominantly concerned with the teaching of craft skills, rather than the development of critical capacity. Teachers rightly argue that students are involved in developing discriminatory and critical skills through the making of art products. However, these are usually in relation to the handling of expressive media, and are not necessarily transferable — particularly to townscape. Allison comments that 'the assumption that aesthetic sensibilities are developed as a consequence of art–making activities has for a long time been a mainstay of art education thinking — presumably its occurrence being seen to be due to some kind of osmosis.'

In terms of final ends, there is a remarkable unanimity. Thus Rudolf Arnheim declares that:

'the ultimate aim of art education is to improve the quality of life . . . to help the individual cultivate a sense of values, to be able to make judgements, exercise self-direction and self-fulfilment'

while from the standpoint of design education, Peter Green suggests that:

'education is concerned with the response we can make to our surroundings. Experience, knowledge and understanding can change the nature of our response. An articulate and responsible active response can only be made by a visually articulate population.'

Unfortunately, it is not at all clear that at the moment we are seriously pursuing such aims. Ken Baynes told us that his conclusion from his own part in the DES-sponsored study of design in general education, conducted at the Royal College of Art, is that:

'we give them a lot of practice in absorbing knowledge, little in reasoning or decision making; hardly any in handling problems of appreciation. The world of children at school is made up of benign problems and the ethic of the classroom is still to know the answer.'

We believe an important contribution of the Project has been to show that, at least in relation to the built environment, art is quite capable of realizing in practice the analytic and critical role foreseen for it by these commentators.

The perceptual domain

Robert Witkin has attempted to explain how the use of expressive media can help the child to organize and understand his experience and how he might communicate this understanding to himself and to others:

'Art is one of the few subjects in the school curriculum where an affective approach to study is valued and where the relationship of the world of the self with the world of objects and events is continually explored. Art education is concerned with the development of the immediate sensuousness as our way of receiving the world, and the processes we use to symbolize, externalize, understand, order, express, communicate and solve its problems. It is located in the belief that visual/tactile ways of knowing/thinking/feeling are one of the most important ways of receiving, organizing, understanding and transmitting impulses, feelings and ideas. It is essentially affective and concerned with the development of visual/tactile values as a means of developing perception.'[3]

This may be considered as an important aspect of environmental education, which involves not only a knowledge of the physical world, but is concerned with attitudes and values, how people feel about their environment, how they relate to it, how they affect it. Witkin says:

'Adaption implies not only that the individual is able to relate one fact to another or to grasp logical sequences. It implies also that the individual is able to relate personally to the world in which he moves.'

A sensory response is the prerequisite of a feeling response. Thus, in terms of environmental education as a whole, Keith Wheeler emphasizes that:

'feelings arise from direct experience, so that any extension of sensitivity requires opportunities to react emotionally and identify with their feelings. To extend sensitivity students need direct experience with objects and people.'[4]

The specific role of the art teacher in this is, in Herbert Read's words:

'to make possible for children an adequate feeling response to the exterior and interior world.'[5]

For many art teachers, however, the experience for which they feel they have a responsibility is experience of expressive media — clay, paint, wood, string and so on. It does not usually mean the development of an active response to environmental stimuli in a wider context. It rarely means the provision of a setting for such a response, or the teacher's involvement in such an experience with the pupil. Many art teachers consider, almost as a matter of faith, that feelings, ideas and impulses should be personal and private to the individual, and should not be interfered with by the art teacher, who is ready to be involved only when the pupil attempts to realise his ideas and needs help in the manipulation of media.

Contrast this passive role with that of the drama teacher who creates an environment calculated to elicit a feeling response, or the music teacher coaxing an interpretation as well as technical fluency out of the student. Witkin observes:

'The art teacher wants to see emotional engagement, but the art lesson is rarely the place where such engagement is actually stimulated as opposed to being passively facilitated. The art teacher tends to be relatively inactive with respect to the pupils' ideas.'[6]

It is not surprising that many pupils still see the art course in terms of making pots, printing fabrics or painting portraits, rather than as the milieu for the discovery, understanding and communication of ideas. Of course the child may learn to pot or paint or print, but he should also be taught to see, and the teacher should also help the development of the pupil's visual language as a way of understanding, feeling and expressing, and of relating this personal development to his everyday world.

This is not a matter of formal lessons about line, colour, tone and texture in the art room, in the hope that pupils will then automatically apply this knowledge to everything they see. It is a matter of learning their vocabulary through direct experience — the impact of the silhouette of an office block, the pattern of the floorscape, the texture of moss on a brick wall. These cannot be learned from someone else's description. They have to be seen, felt, smelled.

It can be argued that the concept of direct experience in art education has to be reconsidered. It is not the experience of materials, of expressive media, that is so important, but the experience of life itself.

The most positive indication that art teachers are beginning to seek their own particular involvement in environmental education is the present strong reaction against the use of second-hand visual reference through looting illustrative images from comics and magazines. There is a swing towards direct experience and observation. Our experience with *Art and the Built Environment* fits naturally into these changing, more positive and active, attitudes to perception.

The expressive domain

Following his work in the Schools Council *Art and the Adolescent* Project Malcolm Ross has made, in his book *The Creative Arts*, a strong case 'to establish the expressive principle as the basis of the arts curriculum as a whole.'[7] He returns constantly to this theme:

'Arts education is about the expressive representation of a child's feelings in private and public form. Our job as teachers of the arts may be quite simply put: to help children master the process of expressive representation.'

He thus justifies much of the work being done in art departments which uses the environment as an inexhaustible source of ideas, as a basis for image making.

It is worth quoting from Ross again to explain the connection between art products and environmental perception, as we have been uncertain as to the value of art products as an indication of increased environmental awareness and perception: 'Through image making we gain access to the world of feeling. Thinking in images is feeling.' This, reassuringly, relates to our aim of developing an increased affective response. Ross declares that 'making sense of experience means acting upon that experience. Representation transforms sensation into perceptual faculties.' This conclusion supports our aims of encouraging an increased awareness and developing environmental perception.

But we wonder if this is entirely adequate, particularly in relation to the wide range of educational responsibilities placed on schools today, and especially in relation to our own Project's aims concerned with the development of critical capacities. For instance Ross's 'manipulation of expressive media', or the role of the artist as teacher, are not a great help so far as critical appraisal of the built environment are concerned. He does mention the possibility that 'impressive forms mirror our experience of the world of objects: through impressive representation we comprehend and find our way in the world.' Perhaps further work should be attempted on the relationship of the language of 'impressive representation' to the language of criticism.

Art teachers often explain their role as that of helping the pupils to express themselves. But it is also important to have something to say. It is not only in experience and analysis of the aesthetics of the built environment that the art teacher has a vital part to play, but also in the synthesis of that experience and understanding; in the realization and communication of the students' perceptions. All those aims like 'self-expression', 'self-understanding', 'self-development' or 'self-awareness' cannot be developed in a vacuum, but are concerned with subjective responses to the external world of ideas, events, people and objects. As Arnheim puts it:

'the self expresses itself most clearly through the dealings with the outer world. There is no psychological justification for the separation of the inner self from the reactions to outer reality.'[8]

A friendly observer from outside the world of art education remarks that:

' "art as expression" which made for riotous success in the infant department, has made it difficult for art to survive in the hard cold education world of the secondary school. Art as perception provides a stronger case for the central position of art in the school curriculum. "Seeing" and "representing" thus become a counterpart of "reading and writing".'[9]

But perhaps the last word on the relationship between expression and perception was said as long ago as 1911 by Edmond Holmes, a famous Inspector of Schools in his day:

'Perception and expression are interdependent. When the child perceives something for himself, he must give his perception some kind of expression, thus representing his experience to himself and to others. When on the other hand, he feels a genuine need to express himself, no matter what the context, it is only because he has perceived something for himself. Perception and expression are not two faculties, but one. Each divorced from the other ceases to be its own true self. When perception is real, living, informed with personal feeling, it must needs find outlet for itself in expression. When expression is real, living, informed with personal feeling, perception — the child's own perception of things — must needs be behind it. Once we realize that expression is the other self of perception, it becomes permissible for us to say that to train the perceptive faculties — the faculties by which man lays hold upon the world that surrounds him and draws it into himself and makes it his own — is the highest achievement of the teacher's art.'[10]

The historical/cultural domain

Few art teachers would say with any confidence that their students' encounters with the built environment enable them 'to realize the historical context of what is encountered' and 'to appreciate the contributions to and functions within, differing cultures and societies' that this particular aspect of art makes.

The DES survey of *Art in Schools*[11] reported that 'it is the exception rather than the rule to find formal courses in art history being given in the 11 to 15 year age range. After that age many of those taking "A" level take a written paper in the history of art or architecture.' Traditionally, examination courses in the history of architecture have followed a chronological sequence of periods and styles, with one particular period given special attention. Whatever the merits of such an approach as a groundwork in architectural history as a formal study, it has severe limitations from the point of view of the Project. It concentrates on particular 'great buildings' ignoring their surroundings of ordinary anonymous townscape, it virtually ignores vernacular architecture, and it ceases at some particular time in the past, ignoring the work of the present century, except, in some syllabuses, certain celebrated masterpieces.

Both teachers and examiners have recognized these limitations, and have given more emphasis to a study of some building or buildings with which the student is personally acquainted. The DES survey noted that:

'some GCE examination syllabuses offer schools the opportunity to include local studies in both fine art, architecture and the general environment. This could well give added incentive and interest to pupils who, for example, may find the study of the buildings in their own town more relevant than a study of those in Athens.'

All examiners we have spoken to have stressed how much they welcome individual studies which bring into the realm of architectural history the 'unpedigreed' architecture of vernacular, industrial and suburban buildings, and how refreshing it is to see work which encompasses the grouping of buildings and the spaces between them. Quite apart from the value of historical or geographical approaches to townscape, its study *as an art form* is an essential component of art education.

Moira Doolar, writing in the context of a visual approach, says:

'there are many ways of studying our environment. It can be studied in terms of all school subjects: history, geography, English, maths, careers. But if an interdisciplinary project is to be of any deep or permanent value, it must have an energizing core. It must be a study of importance to the whole individual, and that means something more than a factual survey or a mental exercise. It must involve the deeper centres of being, from which our feelings and emotions draw their strength. And it must encourage those feelings to emerge and take form in their own way to speak their own language and take on their own shape, which is that of the arts.'

This reference to the 'language of the arts' is important in connection with the historical/cultural domain because, like spoken language, it is both the product and context of culture and history.

Messages are conveyed to us not only through words, but through the visual language of signs and symbols, by the particular form and arrangement of buildings and objects which communicate a wide range of meanings, and encourage certain responses from us. Townscape forms express particular historical and cultural values and relationships which affect our perception of a place. The *Art and the Built Environment* Project is thus concerned not only with the physical environment, but with the meanings and ideas conveyed by particular townscapes. However, perception is dependent not only on visual acuity and our ability to read this visual language, but is influenced by memory, imagination, our knowledge of science, literature or design, the ideas and feelings we project on to the environment, as much as by the messages we receive from it. It is an interdisciplinary phenomenon, an expression of culture and a reality in history.

Jacqueline lake
(Mrs Meredith)

I did not like the colour because it was a shocking pink. There is wire over the door and it looks terrible because it spoils the doors appearance. The attic is very looking from outside but you might have a good view from the inside.

5 The need for critical appraisal

Critic: estimator judge assessor inspector
reporter commentator valuer surveyor appraiser
reviewer theorist hypothesist guesser surmiser
interpreter expositor annotator dissertator
essayist writer publicist man of taste connoisseur

Criticise: sizeup sum up take stock comment
examine investigate ponder evaluate appraise
explain consider elucidate annotate interpret illustrate
define give sense to appreciate discriminate

Roget's Thesaurus

Criticism, for us, as for the lexicographer, implies interpretation and not necessarily disapproval. The point is stressed in environmental terms by the directors of the Open University's *Art and Environment* course, who insist that:

'Just as we cannot stop reading the environment all the time, even when bored by what we read, so we cannot stop evaluating it. True, much of what there is does not register with us consciously — for example, a dull neighbourhood, a banal poster — though it may well act as a background drone. Whatever does register we like or dislike in some degree or respect — or feel indifferent to — which is perhaps a mild form of dislike. Whenever we form judgements of the like/dislike/indifferent kind, we are in the evaluation business, which is to say we are critics, since criticism is nothing more or less than shared evaluation, formulated and communicated.'[1]

Critical study demands not only a response, but a thinking response. It asks you to reflect on your thoughts and feelings, to question experiences, assumptions and meanings, and to communicate your thoughts and conclusions in an appropriate way. It asks you to make considered judgements. Art teachers are familiar with criticism through study of the history of painting and the history of architecture. The place of criticism in education is generally seen in a historic context and implies certain cultural values. Problems arise for schools in the study of contemporary culture which seems to be relevant to the critical study of the environment.

Often teachers attempt to abandon the historical-cultural approach and, to make study more 'relevant', seek areas of which the students have direct experience: the world of popular music, the media and the cults associated with football, motorcycles and clothes. They often feel inadequate because these are areas in which pupils *have* direct experience and opinions, or because the usual critical criteria do not seem to be relevant. The interpretation and evaluation of the environment may offer similar problems and conflicts between teachers and pupils in such matters as interest, experience, taste and perception. Teachers involved in aspects of criticism in other subject areas — English literature for example, and history or social studies — have been striving to get away from the tendency to rely on reference to outside authorities to support arguments and justify opinions. In the critical approach to the built environment which is our concern, the outside authorities have a selection of approaches to draw upon, but no last words. The Project seeks to present students with a range of possibilities to consider, and to encourage them to make up their own minds on the basis of their own experience. This involves personal research, observations, comparisons and conclusions which communicate a considered, personal, critical response. We may approach a critical study of the environment in much the same way as we would approach anything else — a book, a play a film or a painting. Criticism of these does not usually take the form of yet another book, play, film or painting, but necessitates a different kind of statement which explains responses, justifies opinions, notes sources, makes comparisons, establishes relationships, maybe offers alternatives and indicates a personal viewpoint. It gives us a considered appraisal of the thing itself, giving reasons for particular judgements.

We have already mentioned the difficulty that this presents for art departments, geared to the production of art objects which 'legitimize' the activity. There are real difficulties for teachers and pupils alike in tackling work which has a different kind of end product. Sporadic attempts have been made in design education to incorporate criticism and critical studies, generally approached through consumer education or through problem-solving techniques intended to give the pupil the experience of 'being a designer'. In environmental education under other subject headings there has been little evidence of critical studies, apart from the emphasis on environmental problems and the search for solutions. The only area which seems to exploit and develop critical appraisal of the kind we have in mind is that of media studies, usually conducted by English and social studies teachers, an area in which only a few art teachers are marginally involved, and which design teachers seldom consider their field of responsibility, even though advertising and the media are an area where design profoundly affects our lives and decisions.

We have concluded that discriminatory skills will not necessarily develop as a result of producing art objects. Unless specific stimulus, direction and support comes from the art teacher, it is an aspect of work that will be neglected. If art teachers do not choose to involve themselves in the critical appraisal of the built environment, it is unlikely that other subject teachers will. We say this, not to exalt the particular sensitivity of art teachers, but because we have so often met teachers who felt that their own approach *needed* the enhancement which the artist's eye might give. They may have been wrong. They may have been completely equal to the task themselves. We would find it distasteful to suggest that art educators have a wisdom which is denied to others. Nevertheless these other teachers have frequently told us that they have been conscious of a missing element which they have looked to art to provide.

Language

'Unless you define your notes and establish a musical grammar, you will never be able to play a tune, even a simple one, let alone Mozart! . . . the main claim of townscape is that it has assisted in charting the structure of the subjective world. Unless it is charted, to what can you adjust? To opinion, fashions or to a personal morality? How difficult it is to adjust to vagueness and how time-wasting . . .'

GORDON CULLEN, *The Concise Townscape*

One of the most inhibiting factors which has emerged in relation to critical appraisal has been that of language. Art teachers constantly tell us that they are involved with the development of a visual language as a means of expression. Our Project is concerned with developing an understanding of the visual language of townscape, and in evolving appropriate language forms which express a considered, critical response to the experience of townscape.

The Project has encountered difficulty in encouraging students, including A-level Art students, both to make aesthetic judgements and to explain them. Not only have we found students' critical vocabulary generally to be very limited, but art teachers have been reluctant to become involved in areas which demand the use of language forms other than those which employ visual/tactile modes. This is an unnecessarily limited view of art education. We have met, for example, sixth form students, in and out of our Project, who were grateful for the various word lists incorporated in Chapter 8. They discovered, presumably for the first time, these appraisive words and were then anxious to find stronger, more expressive or more precise words, to communicate their responses.

Art teachers are familiar with the notion of art-as-a-language, though perhaps they are more interested in how to say things than in what, or why, one should say them. But the art teacher is well placed to encourage the development of language skills apart from those involved in the emergence of a visual language. There is, and has always been, an enormous scope in the art studio for discussion, explanation, argument and criticism. Sometimes, we would dare to say, it is the only place in the school where these activities happen.

What critical appraisal can be made of a place? What is the basis for the judgements we make? How can we explain our judgements? We have noticed that although people may be capable of making judgements or choices, they are reluctant to question, explain or justify them. To describe something does not necessarily involve critical appraisal. There is an obvious difference between criticism and description. For instance, words like long, short, tall, wide, bright, yellow, are descriptions of physical attributes but are not critical statements. Whereas words like ugly, boring, exciting, monotonous, intrusive, strange, are value-laden and warrant further explanation. What are the factors that contribute to feelings of excitement, interest, enclosure, boredom or beauty in relation to a particular townscape? How can townscape be analysed to identify these various elements? How can this information be synthesized to explain the complex relationship that exists between the various elements and between them and the observer? What are the factors that affect perception?

Artist and critic

The attempt to answer these questions involves a visual language, both in terms of understanding the townscape experience itself, and in terms of its evaluation. But a successful explanation requires more. It needs, in addition, written or spoken language. It is clear that criticism is not restricted to the visual but needs to employ a number of modes of communication.

In relation to townscape, both the artist and critic are grappling with the problems of understanding a visual language. They are both engaged in the experience of visual/tactile stimuli, in the observation and understanding of townscape, in making judgements about it. The artist works through visual imagery, and is not required to explain his judgements, whereas the critic is bound to offer explanation, which is where the use of other forms of language becomes necessary.

The response of many students was primarily that of the artist. But we were also asking for another kind of perception: a specific critical response to particular situations — a curving street, a quiet cul-de-sac, a shopping parade, a school playground. What properties do these possess which contribute to a particular quality of place? How might they be described? How might they be assessed?

Perception is a creative act. The modes adopted by the artist and the critic may be different, but both involve a creative response. In neither case is this merely absorption and regurgitation of information. Both involve highly complex acts of scanning, selecting, observing, analysing, categorizing, comparing, establishing relationships between the familiar and the unfamiliar. There is no absolute reality to which we respond. All the time we are projecting feelings, ideas, values onto the environment as well as receiving sensations and messages from it. We are all the time creating and recreating our own reality. The artist and the critic do not differ in this.

There are various ways of perceiving which can encompass a whole range of interpretations, opinions and points of view. We should emphasize that in comparing the view of the artist with that of the critic, we are not saying that one is subjective and the other objective. In the context of the Project they are both subjective responses realized in different ways. The artist works through visual imagery, his feelings, thoughts and ideas are implicit in his work, and the onus is on the observer to interpret the artist's meaning. However, the critic is obliged to make his meaning explicit, so there can be no doubt what his judgements and opinions are. This is why the use of a verbal or written language is necessary.

Participation

The development of critical awareness is a desirable end in itself. But it is also vital if we are ever to have effective public participation in the making of decisions about the environment. It is over a decade since the publication of the Skeffington Report with its aspirations for a creative and participatory role for ordinary people in the planning process, and it is sobering to reflect on how far we are from that goal. In one of his reports on the Educational Priority Project in Liverpool, Dr Eric Midwinter, referring to what he calls the planners' lip-service to consultation, remarked:

'they may knock on the door of a client for rehabilitation or decantation and ask what sort of home and environment is required. What is the unfortunate interviewee to say in answer to this? What in too many cases he could say is something like this, "I was never educated to listen to that kind of question nor to articulate responses, technical or creative, to it".'[2]

There are a number of explanations for the failure of attempts to evolve a participatory system of planning, and they range from the power of entrenched vested interests to the nature of local government bureaucracies. But undoubtedly one major reason is public apathy and ignorance. The apathy is born of resignation: the assumption that the consultation procedure is simply a public relations exercise to legitimize decisions already made. The ignorance is the result of our lack of attention to environmental issues and values in the education system.

The professionals, architects and planners may have a lot to answer for, but key decisions are made by laymen. Councillors who sit on planning committees decide on planning issues. Like the rest of us they have been ill-educated to cope with the problems that face them. They have to do the best they can, but often it is not good enough.

The fact is that responsibility for the environment rests neither with the professionals nor with the councillors. It is the shared responsibility of all of us. We live in it, we pay for it, and we should take a more active and creative part in shaping it to our liking. But what scope is there for people to influence their environment? For some it is confined to wallpapering the front room or digging the garden. But our efforts to shape our surroundings should not stop at the garden gate. The possibilities and the potential, as well as the responsibilities, are much greater than this.

It was not a zealot of community action, but the government's chief planner, who recently declared that:

'People have many different perspectives on their environment and on community life but only now are we beginning to see these articulated. It is not all that many years ago since people trusted local or central government to analyse their problems and prescribe the solutions. Those were the days when people accepted that new and exciting developments were bound to be better and when change seemed to be welcomed. We then moved into a period when unique prescriptive solutions gave way to the presentation of alternatives so that the public could express views before final decisions were taken. Today we face a different situation. Community groups, voluntary organizations of many kinds, and indeed individuals, now demand a say in the definition of problems and a role in determining and

then implementing solutions. Even in the professional field that we normally think of as part of the establishment there are various movements concerned with reinterpreting or changing the professionals' role. Self-help groups of many kinds have sprung up, sometimes around a professional, or, at least, advised or guided by a professional. It is quite clear that a number of people believe that the traditional professionals are not able adequately to communicate with people in a way that will help them solve their problems or make their wishes known to those who take the decisions.'[3]

These changed assumptions about the making of environmental decisions present yet another challenge to the education system. The chief planner uses the word 'articulated'. It may sound like jargon but it is important. Articulation — 'talking about' in the broadest sense — means familiarity with an appropriate language. Participation in discussions of the quality of the built environment depends, in the end, on the ability, first, to read the visual language of buildings and places and, second, to use the visual and verbal language of criticism. The more specific participatory and political skills probably fall in subject areas outside the art studio, but art teachers have a prime responsibility in the development of experiential, perceptual, analytical, critical and communicatory skills. Critical appraisal is for everyone.

A critical approach to townscape

It is one thing to demand that schools should encourage the critical appraisal of the built environment, quite another explain clearly what such a study could be about. What, in short, did our approach to townscape imply about its content and the possibility of interpreting it? In the Project, we were fortunate in being able to draw on the experience of our consultative committee. Keith Wheeler, Brian Goodey and Jeff Bishop demonstrated their approaches in practical terms by producing trial materials for use in schools. The results of this aspect of their work can be seen in Part Two. However, they also contributed to our discussions of more basic principles. Because the idea of appraising the environment critically is unfamiliar, it is worth while setting out briefly something of this background thinking.

Keith Wheeler likens townscape to a maze or labyrinth. Something enigmatic at first but which yields up its secret to exploration:

'Think of a city and you can probably think of a townscape image which sums up the character of the place. For example, Edinburgh has its castle; London, maybe is represented by Tower Bridge; Liverpool has Pier Head, Blackpool its tower, and so on. But what symbol would you choose to express the essence of the urban environment as it is experienced in all its complexity? That is not such an easy question to answer. My choice is the abstract shape of the maze or labyrinth. It is an intricate, involved pattern resembling the choreography of a dance, guiding those who learn to follow its path. It is, according to scholars, an urban symbol, standing for many levels of experience: physical and psychological. We may lose ourselves in the enigma of the maze and find a route to self-discovery. Similarly, our towns and cities are laid out in a series of paths between buildings: passing along these routeways, on foot or by car, brings us up against the built paradox of time and space expressing the human condition. In other words, ''the shaping of space which goes on in architecture and, therefore, in the city, is symbolic of our culture, symbolic of our aspirations, our needs, and our fears.''[4] Churches, factories, houses, institutions, palaces, schools, fortresses, buildings of all kinds and their relationship to each other; monuments, statues, and all kinds of urban paraphernalia; open spaces and waste spaces — all of these combine to make a setting for the human drama played out in the urban theatre we have created for ourselves. Hence, wherever we are in a built environment, some kind of townscape confronts us: an urban scenery we make, not necessarily by conscious choice, but by inevitable collusion with the culture into which we are born.

Townscape is the product of many shaping influences. For example, the relief of the land, or local climate, may determine the urban layout. Even more important are the numerous economic and political decisions made by society and by individuals which are translated into the spatial deployment and appearance of the buildings we inhabit, whether in a barriada in South America, a point block development in London, or a suburb of Los Angeles. Or, on the one hand there is the grand gesture of city design resulting in a Paris or Peking while on the other there is the slow accumulation of buildings over time fitting a domestic scale of urban living, such as an English market town like Woodbridge, Suffolk. But whatever form it takes, townscape inevitably mirrors the life-style of the people who create it, affecting and reflecting human relationships. Hence, townscape is the visual manifestation of the way we put together our architectural surroundings, and in so far as a town or city is an artefact, so townscape is an art form.'

There is in this analysis of Wheeler's the clear suggestion that although it may be enigmatic, townscape is, in fact, quite capable of being understood. He insists on the importance of experience. This comes first. But the experience can be interpreted. The streets and buildings can be made to reveal their meaning. A striking aspect of the Project is that it shows how successful at reading and evaluating these meanings people can be when they have at their disposal appropriate means of approach.

Brian Goodey also emphasizes the primacy of experience and has championed the idea of the 'sensory walk' as a way of deliberately seeking out, collecting and evaluating environmental perceptions:

'Knowledge comes to us in two ways — through our intellectual pursuit and understanding, and through our direct experience. Often our eyes are closed to the obvious by our overuse of one system rather than another. If we are too open to experiences we may never see the wood for trees, if we are too tightly controlled by our intellect we may never get to share the vision, insight or awareness of the artist or poet.

The sensory walk is an opportunity to look again at a familiar environment, and at the same time to re-examine how you see the world. Do you see it through your emotions or through your intellect?

Creativity is the constant interplay between intuition and rationality. If we are to become aware of ourselves and our environment and if we are to try to deal with man and his problems, creatively, we must begin at the level of our own perceptual processes.'

Once again the practical success of the sensory walk idea in the Project is proof that these aspects of perception and their critical interpretation are open to deliberate development by teaching and learning.

Jeff Bishop is an architect and his particular insight is to make a relationship between the work of educational theorists like Piaget and architectural commentators such as Norberg-Schulz and Kevin Lynch. He identifies Piaget's pre-school period as a crucial one in the emergence and subsequent growth of environmental awareness:

'This stage, usually connected with children of 3-7 years old, is the period of ''Topological Space'', when the child structures spatial relationships around ''elementary'' perceptions of: 1 Proximity; 2 Separation; 3 Order (or spatial succession); 4 Enclosure or surrounding; 5 Continuity. I do not wish to enlarge upon these categories but merely to make two points. Firstly, it is not (I suspect) coincidental that Topology is now not an elementary branch of mathematics but an extremely progressive and advanced one. Secondly, Moore points out that a person experiencing novel environments appears to construe them through topological elements regardless of that person's stage of development . . .'

He goes on:

'We cannot escape space so we structure it and invest it with meanings. After Piaget the second most important source is Christian Norberg-Schulz, an architectural historian and theorist. In two books *Existence, Space and Architecture*[5] and *Meaning in Western Architecture*[6] he explores and develops his concept of the fundamental elements in our structuring of space. These elements he terms Place, Path and Domain. The first two should be self-explanatory, the third is related to the way we divide up and attribute space to functions, people or symbolic elements. Norberg-Schulz sees these in all major architectural works including those of the present. His work has stimulated others to explore similar territory, notably Ivor Smith, Head of the School of Architecture at Bristol University. Smith defines five elements — Context, Routes, Environment, Interface and Grouping. I personally tend to exclude Environment (the control of heat, light and sound) not because it is unimportant but because it is of a different order to the rest. 'Routes' clearly relates to Norberg-

Schulz's 'Path', 'Grouping' to 'Domain', and 'Context' is the negative of 'Place' for, as Norberg-Schulz says, 'the fact that the concept of *place* implies an inside and an outside makes it clear that the *place* is situated within a larger context and cannot be understood in isolation'. This leaves 'interface' which I fully accept as an important addition to the place/path/domain group but which I shall not discuss further here, because there is another major source to mention along with Norberg-Schulz — Kevin Lynch.

Lynch derived, from analysis of a number of freehand maps of cities, his own set of elements by which he suggests people structure their mental images of the environment. These elements he calls Nodes, Landmarks, Edges, Routes and Districts and with the exception of Edges it is easy to see the relationship between his terms and those of Norberg-Schulz, (one can consider Nodes and Landmarks to be broadly similar locational elements). It is then possible to relate all the terms so far introduced in a diagram as follows:

Piaget	*Norberg-Schulz*	*Smith*	*Lynch*
Proximity	Place	Context	Node/Landmark
Sequence	Path	Routes	Routes
Enclosure	Domain	Grouping	District'

At this point Jeff Bishop points out Herbert Read's insistence that 'childish' modes of perception are not discarded because they are superseded by more 'adult' modes. They continue to be important personally and culturally for the grown-up person. Bishop asserts that this 'topological' grouping is, in fact, essential to all perceptions of architecture and is basic to any attempt to encourage involvement with the built environment. The elements underlie the approaches to critical appraisal used in the Project and their success is surely connected with the possibility of a firm psychological basis in child development.

There can hardly be a final word on what can be appraised and understood in the built environment. The extension of that range is a creative part of critical and educational activity, always being enlarged. We saw this in action in our trial schools and, more recently in the first inter-disciplinary working parties. All were quite able to suggest their own approaches and to devise their own study methods to get at what they wanted to understand about buildings and places. It is, on the other hand, important to find that it is possible to reach agreement on the fundamental nature of architectural perceptions and on the permanence of the spatial, tactile and other qualities that are there to be evaluated in everything that men have made.

Part Two:
The study methods

EASEL

UMBRELLA

SKETCH PAD

NUMEROUS BRUSHES, PENS, PENCILS

INSIDE :-
· FOLD. UP CHAIR
· FLASK
· LUNCH BOX
· (RAINCOAT)
· WRITING PAPER
· CHANGE OF WALKING SHOES

TAPE RECORDER + MANY TAPES

GOOD & EXPENSIVE CAMERA

BAG :- BOOKS ON TOWNSCAPE, DRAWING, LITTLE NOTE BOOK FOR PHOTOS.
· VIEWFINDER
· MAP

The study methods

It is intended that teachers should modify, adapt, add to and sometimes reject the methods described here. They are offered as a basis for studying the environment using techniques familiar in other aspects of art education. The majority of teachers will want to make full use of the suggestions relating them to their own situation and to the age and ability of the children.

The following study methods on EXPERIENCING, ANALYSING and APPRAISING townscape are derived from the Project's research in schools and with teachers' groups. A number of them have been influenced by the work of Gordon Cullen, while others are derived from contributions by Jeff Bishop, Brian Goodey and Keith Wheeler, who prepared materials for use in the Project trial schools.

The particular approaches described here are not an exhaustive or comprehensive collection, but merely illustrate early attempts during the Project's research to extend students' capacities to experience, understand and evaluate environmental quality. For ease of reference, they are listed in a particular order, but it should be understood that they are interactive, and also may be easily adapted to suit varying age groups.

The aim of the study methods is to develop a sense of place. 'A place is a piece of the whole environment which has been claimed by feelings.' The concern has been to encourage an adequate feeling response and to extend students' powers of discrimination and judgement.

The whole thrust of the exercises is to help elicit a personal emotional response, to help pupils describe their experience, to articulate their judgements and explain their views.

6 Introducing ABE work in class

The purpose of an introduction should be to interest and excite the pupils, to prepare them to explore, observe, appraise and comment. Other aspects of both art and environmental study provide them with a basis for learning. The value of ABE work is that it is derived from their own experience, based on knowledge gained at first hand, and reliant upon their expertise to interpret and communicate.

An important part of the introduction is that it can set the pattern for a particular set of attitudes to learning. Here we are looking for curiosity, enquiry and a healthy scepticism about received opinion. There is also the point that because every environment is unique the pupils are as much experts on it as the teacher. Teacher and pupils must engage in a cooperative venture involving direct experience and its interpretation. This means that the most useful model for the pupils is that of the 'good learner' and, from the start, it is up to the teacher to demonstrate by example what this implies.

Slide programmes as an introduction

It is important to present a lively introduction to the study, offering a lot of visual stimulus, and there are many slide packs already on the market which might serve the purpose — as long as the teacher is prepared to adapt them to the particular needs of the pupils.

The Project Team has prepared three filmstrips (published by Longman for the Schools Council) — *Approaches to Townscape, A Personal Response* and *A Critical Response* — as a general introduction to the work of the Project. But, like other commercial products, they can only be second best to the stimulus offered by the local area itself. Teachers and pupils can devise their own learning resources, and by so doing, develop the study they are trying to promote.

There is no mystique to making a slide programme. Anyone who can take holiday snaps is capable of putting together a sequence of photographic images designed to tell a story. What is important is the ideas and concepts they illustrate rather than the technical finish.

The value of the teacher producing a programme of this kind is that it shows how generalizations about buildings apply to particular places that are local and well-known. As a result children can relate the wider context to their own experience.

Any area will provide good material for a slide programme. Every town, village or estate contains elements for appreciation, criticism and design. The following storyboard offers the basis for a typical script and shows the range of topics that might be included.

STORYBOARD · SLIDE PROGRAMME

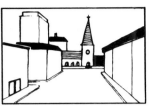

buildings

spaces
messages

streetscape
routes
meeting points
shops

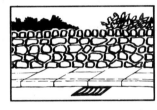

vocabulary
line tone colour
texture pattern
mass volume scale
etc.

vocabulary
balance articulation
proportion enclosure
contrast symmetry
decoration rhythm

barriers
physical
visual
psychological

natural form

people
personalisation

Journey to school as an introduction

The daily journey to school offers an excellent starting point. To view it analytically means looking afresh at a familiar experience which we tend to take for granted and this is possibly one of the most difficult things to achieve. Yet it is central to the Project.

Pupils are asked to describe through words and pictures their journey. This brings into focus things which are important to children and offers the teacher an insight into the level and quality of their experiences and perceptions. Initially the study will show pupils that memory needs to be supplemented by observation, and this will be an introduction to the deliberate study of the built environment.

mental maps

Teachers' mental maps of Buxton indicate their knowledge of the town before attempting their townscape study. Such maps may identify elements and relationships evident and important to the perceiver, and can offer a worthwhile starting point for streetwork.

Of course, it is useful to repeat the exercise after the study to find out how perceptions have been modified.

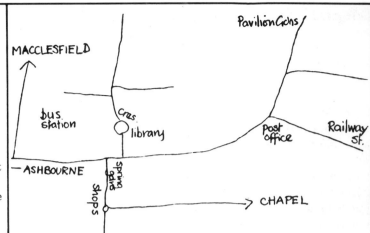

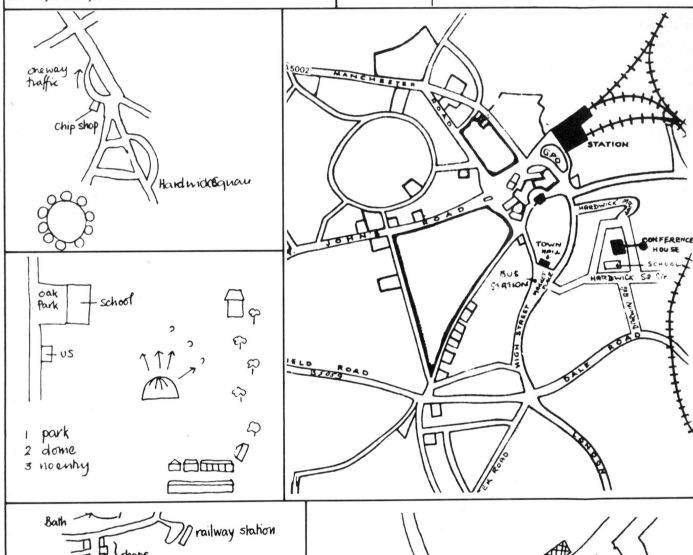

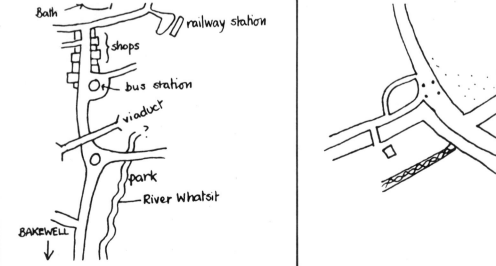

Mental maps as an introduction

The basis of the work is children's experience of the environment. Looking out of a window from a bus or at photographs are not enough in themselves, though they are activities which might be included in a longer term study. We have found that many teachers tend to work not from the children's experience or understanding of an area, but from their own perceptions, which may be very different from those of their pupils. Or else, they might wish to transmit their own views of what is good, bad or indifferent, which is not the same as encouraging the pupils to develop their own powers of discrimination and judgement.

Mental maps, which are maps of familiar places made from memory, are a good way of reminding pupils that they already know a great deal about the area. They are the experts on the local environment. They know the neighbourhood in a different way from their teachers, and have gained insight through their own direct experience of living there. This should not only be recognized, but exploited. We should seek to build on a basis of pupils' knowledge rather than on their ignorance, which is so often the starting point for learning in schools. It is much sounder educational practice to start from where we are than merely regurgitate what the teacher tells us.

Of course this is a very useful diagnostic device. It will provide the teacher with a valuable starting point because through discussion of the maps, he or she will share with the pupils an understanding of where they live. It will indicate how partial this understanding is, and therefore provide a basis for further study.

Rod shapes
skyline.
↑
↓
people / cars
signs / seats

Scale of cars + people emphasis distance
also narrowing space receding towards archway.
colours soon less importants than dark + light shapes
splitting up large shapes.
eg. traffic sign. + heads compare.
clock + roof shapes dominant.
people loom towards you cutting out vision. below eyelevel.
a feeling of constant movement because I am static.

7 Experiential and perceptual skills

The value of exploiting first-hand environmental experience as a basis for learning is that it is the richest and most widely available resource that we have. To profit from it, children need help to develop their capacity to respond to environmental stimuli, to be open to new experience, to be prepared for it, to be receptive to the rich variety of sensory experience the environment has to offer. Teachers need to find ways of extending, deepening or changing children's experience of the environment, and to work towards heightening sensitivity, enlarging sensory perception and thus developing a greater awareness of the environment.

The following study methods attempt to do this — by encouraging a greater dependence on the use of all the senses; and by emphasizing the need for emotional response.

Teachers wishing to stimulate their students' sensory perception of the built environment need to break through the inhibitions associated with subjective learning and the education of the emotions. Much of our cultural training suppresses this aspect of our personalities so that by adolescence young people are either too shy to express themselves in this way, or their minds are only geared to fact-oriented problems. The various techniques suggested here are a means of leading students to respond to the built environment, and describe what they feel.

Loosening up

Sensing the environment requires us to be *open* to what the environment has to offer. Schools are seldom 'open' settings for receiving sensory stimuli and the nature of timetabling may mean that sensory experiences are sandwiched between formal learning experiences, full of social rules. Teacher and pupils may want to try a few loosening up exercises which serve to mark the environmental experience off from normal time and place — some of the techniques developed in educational drama can be used if the teacher feels familiar and confident with this kind of approach.

There are many different ways of loosening the senses. One way is to encourage their more effective use by removing one sense so that greater reliance is placed on another. Some exercises, like the 'feely bag' where objects are encountered by touch alone, are already well-known to teachers.

Here is another example of a 'loosening' exercise: Using pairs of students, and ensuring that the area to be used is free of obvious hazards, get one member of each pair to either close eyes or be blindfolded. The blindfolded person then reports initial sensings to the other. Given a degree of trust and responsibility, the 'sighted' person can then guide the 'blind' person along a route which may take in sounds, smells, textures and experiences. The pair should then switch roles. Discussion and de-briefing of this experience inevitably leads to consideration of the problems of the blind, but it must be taken beyond this to the student's own experiences of the environment, and of the partner in whom trust was placed. A similar exercise can be done with wheelchairs where it is the sense of movement and mobility which is cut off.

Sensory walk

Brian Goodey says that a sensory walk is an

'experiential guide to the local environment' inviting 'the user to experience something in a series of places . . . There are no specific features for observation, rather is the walk a "tuning-in" to the environment.'

In the form shown here, it has been used in primary and secondary schools and on teachers' courses. Among its effects are a reminder to the participants that the environment is experienced and perceived through all the senses.

This exercise can be done either on a predetermined route or as an individual exploration.

Score

An environmental 'score' may be attempted, based on the ideas of Lawrence Halprin, an American landscape architect, who sets out to encourage public participation in planning. His answer is to encourage a set of purposeful environmental explorations during which 'untrained' observers can experience and evaluate their everyday surroundings.

Central to Halprin's ideas is the concept of a 'score', which like a musical score, or the work of John Cage, structures the user's activities, but allows room for improvisation. In the context of an environmental score, the main aim of the operation must be, as Halprin notes, 'STOP, LOOK AND LISTEN' and to 'RECORD our feelings.' His approach is exemplified in the score he produced for the town of Everett in the United States.

where did you go ?	what were you reminded of ?
	what was your funniest thought ?
	what was your strangest thought ?

what did you taste ?	what did you smell ?

what did you hear ?	what did you feel ?

?

what words did you encounter?
(spoken · written)

what did you see ? (graphic answers only)

Leave the building. Note your first impressions – (weather, smells, movement, feelings) Amble for three minutes. Stop. Compare this place with when you first stepped into the street. Continue walking but allow yourself to be attracted by other roads, alleyways, shop windows, doorways, inviting spaces, arresting details – anything that interests you. Chart your route.
Note reasons for changes in course, reasons for pausing. Continue for five minutes. Change your pace. Find a place that makes you happy; one that disturbs you; afraid; at peace;
Note the elements that contribute to these feelings.

Search for a place where you can sit in complete silence for three minutes. Close your eyes. Soak up the sounds, smells, vibrations and any other sensations. Record your impressions by (truthfully) noting the first thirty words you think of.

Choose a building where people are going out and in. How do they behave in relation to the building? How do they approach it? How do they leave? What can you guess from their behaviour?

Change direction. Find places that are beautiful; crowded; bright; spot something you have never noticed before. Find the shortest route between you and your starting point. Note as many sensations, images, details as you can – buildings, spaces, people, colour, light, textures, sounds, smells, incidents, messages, thoughts, feelings, memories. Describe your experience.

The Everett Walk

Colby & Hewitt (street intersection)

— Walk around the intersection and observe the movement of autos and people and the activities taking place here.
— Stop two separate people and ask directions to the waterfront. Ask what there is to see and do there.
— Close your eyes for one minute and listen to the sounds of the city.
— Record which location within this intersection, if any, that you liked best. Which did you like least?

Hewitt, block W. of Colby

— Walk the block.
— Record in what ways this block differs in feeling from an adjacent block on Colby.

Alley between Hewitt & Wall, W. of Colby

— Walk the alley to mid-point.
— Close your eyes for one minute and listen to the sounds of this place in the city.
— How does this place make you feel?
— Can you identify three buildings which front on Colby?

Colby & Pacific

— Observe Colby to the north and to the south.
— Record your dominant impressions of this street. What do you like about the street? What do you not like?

Forecourt of County Courthouse

— Take a seat and observe the human activities taking place in, and the physical characteristics of, the forecourt.
— How does the place feel to you?
— From the western portion of the forecourt observe the activities adjacent to the intersection of Wall and Wetmore end and the general view of the northwest.
— What of the things you see would you like to change? What would you retain?
— Walk to the intersection of Rockefeller and Wall. Observe the views to the north and east.
— When the County Courthouse complex is extended to the block east of Rockefeller, what kinds of uses and activities *not* taking place in the present forecourt would you like to see included in the resulting expansion?

Hewitt, block between Rockefeller & Oakes

— Walk the block on both sides of the street. Was there any difference in feeling between the two sides?
— Stop a person and ask what lies to the east of Hewitt and what there is to see and do there.

Roof of Bon Marche parking structure

— Record your dominant impressions of the views, including human activities, to the east and to the southwest. What do you like about these views? What do you not like?

Alley, E. of Colby, between Hewitt & Cal

— From the point opposite the drive-through of Everett Trust observe all the activities you can see taking place.
— How does this place feel to you?
— Walk through Colby and record your experience as a pedestrian.

After walk

— Record on the map and give brief explanation for each:
• Your favourite place in the downtown (mark with an X).
• Your favourite spot on this walk, if different (mark with an O).
• What you consider to be the limits of 'downtown' (mark with a dashed line).
• What you consider to be the centre or centres of 'downtown' (mark in any appropriate way).

This American example can easily be translated into other situations. Teachers should attempt to compose their own scores and these should be suitable both for the particular situation and the children.

The activities that might be involved in composing a score include:

— Begin to LOOK UP as you walk. Notice sky, clouds, treetops, perimeters of buildings, other structures overhead.
— LOOK DOWN for a while; what do you notice underfoot? (textures, surfaces, edges, etc).
— Take a block to walk VERY FAST — end it in a RUN. How does this affect your perception of where you are? Stay with your partner.
— Take a section to walk VERY VERY SLOWLY. Let your path meander in and around. What do you notice at this pace?
— STOP at an intersection. Notice the choreography of all moving elements for a while. Velocities. Rhythms. Interesting actions. A chance dance.
— Tune in to the architecture around you. Pick two details that you would like to sketch later, or remember.
— How are changes in scale affecting you emotionally?
— Which surprises absolutely drew you off your intended path?
— HAVE YOU FOUND ANY OBJECTS YET?

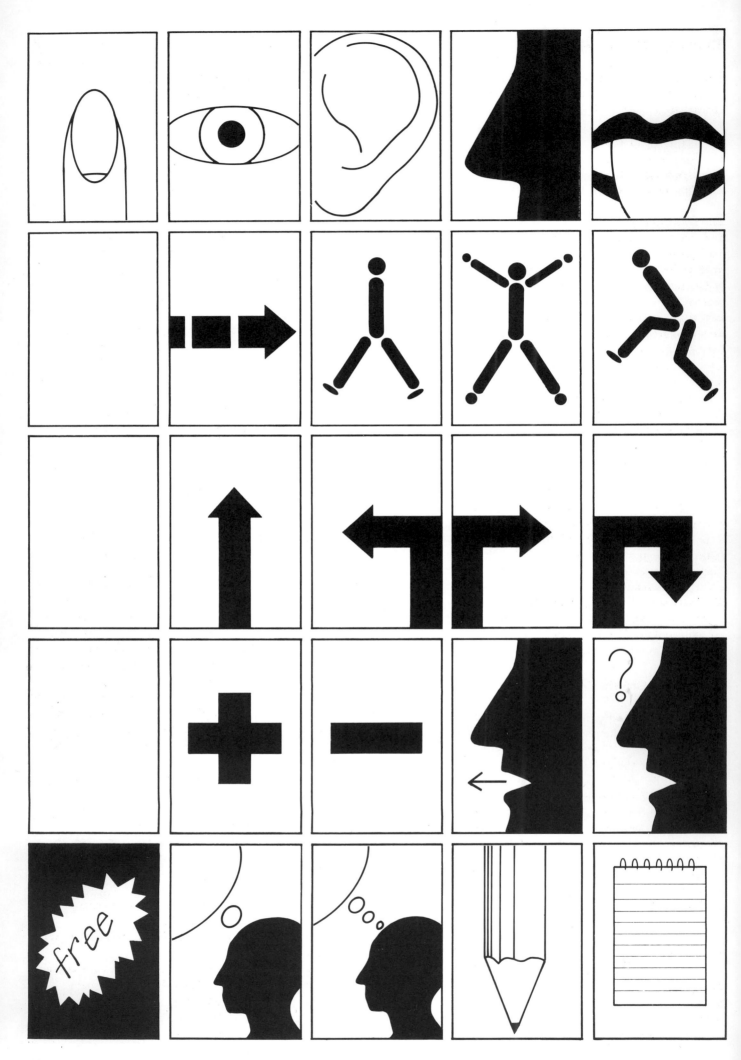

Steering by cards

One of the major problems of sensory walks is their unstructured nature. To get round this problem the Project used *Steering by cards.* Its aims were:

1   To prepare an appropriate set of direction cards for use by each student or student group.
2   To test sets of cards in the local environments reporting on both the environments experienced and the effectiveness of the card sets.

The illustration shows a set of 21 *symbols* which were designed to serve as a repertoire for the activity. Many teachers will want to develop further cards or question and modify the suitability of the designs.

The purpose of the symbols — when enlarged and reproduced on card — is to serve as a random guidance system for a sensory walk. Students take their cue from each card revealed in the shuffled pack. The size and balance of a pack will depend on the interests of individual teachers and the setting in which they are used, and timing and distance cards (or instructions) may be added.

In experimental runs with this technique, it was found that the 5 'sensing' cards and the concluding *Ask, Tell, Draw* and *Write* cards should predominate in any pack, the 'movement' cards being used less frequently unless a large area is to be covered.

The 'sensing' cards should predominate and although they can be used in equal numbers, one sense can obviously be emphasized. *See* cards might well be restricted in favour of *Touch* or *Taste.* The appearance of a 'sensing' card at the top of the pack should act as a switch to the appropriate sense . . . HEAR paper rustling, birds, car doors, children shouting; SMELL chimney smoke, pipe smoke, chips frying, cement, diesel fumes; TOUCH smooth glass, polished brass, gravel, peeling paintwork: TASTE your lips, newsprint, a blade of grass, a chocolate bar. The aim is to experience and not necessarily to record: only record if a *Draw* or *Write* card follows.

Imagine and *Stretch* are similar cards; both involve extending oneself beyond normal activity. *Stretch* is probably the easier as it invites the user to stretch the body, or part of the body and to experience the novelty — jumping to grab a branch, standing on tiptoe to see over a wall, inhaling deeply, throwing the head back to view the sky. *Imagine* is an offer, an offer to explore the mind. Imagine if that man there were actually a secret agent or a retired soccer star, imagine if he/she were to walk over here and chat me up, imagine if I could paint that wall in glorious technicolour, imagine if everything in that shop were free!

The movement and direction symbols are fairly obvious — they provide a random pattern for getting around the area selected.

Move suggests motion up or down, or in any chosen direction, *walk* and *run* are obvious, although of course *run* should be used with care in traffic areas. The direction signs can refer to any level or interval of route as suggested by the teacher e.g. only roads, or roads and paths, or movement in open spaces such as a park or playing field.

Add and *Take* can raise problems, but are not intended to do so! In adding to the environment the user might push a swing, open a gate or chalk a mark. In taking, it is the 'found objects' of the streets or countryside that are suggested — leaves, stones, building debris, printed material and the stuff of which collage is made. The success of those two cards will depend very much on the interpretative advice offered.

Ask and *Tell* imply communication with people *en route,* the gathering of experiences and the passing on of information. Questions should flow easily, but what do you tell? Most people perceive little of their surroundings, and the invitation to look at something, to share an experience with a newcomer can often be welcomed. Again, a certain amount of background work will be required . . .

The use of *Draw* or *Write* will depend very much on the needs of the teacher — our own emphasis has been in experiencing, rather than recording, but if the card walk is to be used as a basis for further work, then a notebook or sketch pad may be mandatory with *Draw* or *Write* included after card drawn.

Free is the joker. The cards are a compromise between free experience and the Pied Piper trails of traditional geography and tourism. The *Free* card should remind the user that he is in control and can experience anything at anytime *en route.*

Steeplechasing

> Combray at a distance was no more than a church epitomizing the town, representing it, speaking of it and for it to the horizon.
>
> MARCEL PROUST

There are few urban areas in Britain which do not possess churches with steeples, spires or towers. They are often marvellous focal points in the townscape, whether they be magnificent medieval spires like St Mary Redcliffe in Bristol, or more humble Victorian versions in the 19th century suburb. Such is the medieval steeple to the church of St Peter in the suburb of Oadby, Leicester. This is something to make pupils consciously aware of townscape by showing them how to enjoy the changing relationship of the steeple to its surroundings as they move about it; glimpsing it from many different points in the streets around it; coming across it unawares in juxtaposition with other buildings; and as they work in a spiral towards it, noting the change in perspective relationship as they move nearer, and becoming more conscious of its balanced mass thrusting to the sky and towering above them. It is the essence of townscape enjoyment. The pleasure of observing the steeple in this way cannot be described: it can only be experienced.

Here is one way to do it:

1   Pupils are asked to find 6 different spaces from which the steeple can be seen.
2   They are asked to spend 5 minutes in each space and to record through annotated sketches the space between them and the steeple.
3   They are finally asked to choose the space they like the best and the least and to explain why.

STEEPLECHASING IN OADBY AN EXPERIENCE OF SERIAL VISION

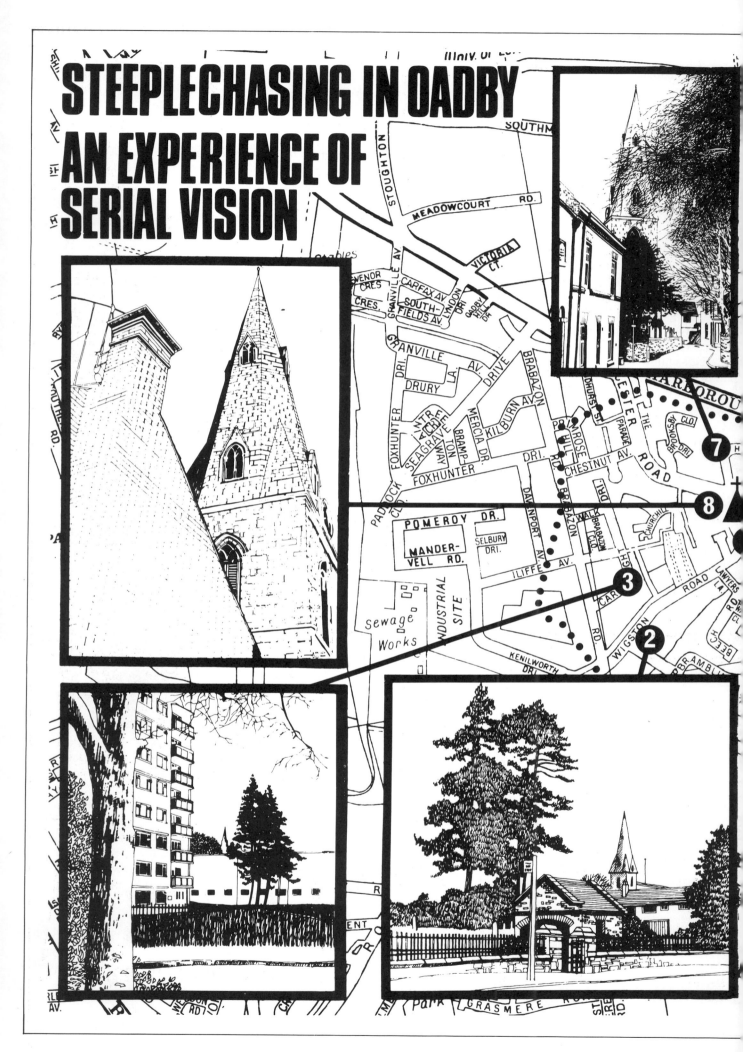

—⑥ **Site of drawing**

···· **Sound boundary**

N

Serial vision

Gordon Cullen says that we understand space not merely by looking at it but by moving through it. Townscape, therefore, is not a collection of static tableaux: it is made up of a continuum of spatial awareness where our perceptions are influenced by what we have experienced and what we expect to experience. Serial vision is a way of revealing this phenomenon.

Cullen explains the activity in this way:

'Let us suppose that we are walking through a town: here is a straight road off which is a courtyard at the far side of which another street leads out and bends slightly before reaching a monument. Not very unusual. We take this path and our first view is that of the street. Upon turning into the courtyard the new view is revealed instantaneously at the point of turning, and this view remains with us while we walk across the courtyard. Leaving this courtyard we enter the further street. Again a new view is suddenly revealed although we are travelling at a uniform speed. Finally, as the road bends, the monument swings into view. The significance of all this is that although the pedestrian walks through the town at a uniform speed, the scenery of the town is often revealed in a series of jerks and revelations. This we call SERIAL VISION.'

from *The Concise Townscape*

Serial vision sequence by Mitzi Sims (Priory School, Portsmouth).

8 Language skills

Jerome Bruner says that 'the child sees the world differently through the use of language which reorders his experience' and concludes, 'the limits of my language are the limits of my world.' The Project revealed that most people's schooling leaves them with an inadequate vocabulary, verbal or visual, for understanding the reality of aesthetic experience. The situation is not helped by the obscurity of the language used by professional critics and by the limited view of what can be considered as 'art' or 'architecture'.

In order to introduce townscape as an area worthy of study, we found that it was necessary to take deliberate action to counterbalance this lack of a language. At the most basic level it was even important to introduce visual and verbal vocabularies.

Words

We are all capable of using words to label aesthetic and design elements in our surroundings. We recognize, describe and evaluate, but seldom do it with any degree of accuracy or subtlety. The purpose of extending ability in this area is to refine and sharpen our critical response. The following word lists have been used effectively to widen students' vocabularies:

Vocabulary derived from Gordon Cullen's The Concise Townscape.

PLACE	CONTENT	FUNCTION
possession	juxtaposition	structures
advantage	immediacy	barriers
viscosity	thisness	steps
enclaves	detail	black and white
enclosure	secrecy	solid and void
focal point	urbanity	texture
precinct	intricacy	lettering
indoor landscape	propriety	trim
outdoor room	bluntness and vigour	roads
multiple enclosure	entanglement	kinetic unity
insubstantial space	nostalgia	public and private
defining space	exposure	water
looking out	intimacy	
thereness	illusion	
here and there	metaphor	
pinpointing	tell tale	
truncation	animism	
change of level	absence	
netting	significant objects	
silhouette	building as sculpture	
grandiose vista	geometry	
division of space	multiple use	
handsome gesture	foils	
closed vista	relationships	
deflection	scale	
projection and recession	distortion	
incident	natural form	
punctuation	calligraphy	
narrows	publicity	
fluctuation		
undulation		
closure		
recession		
anticipation		
infinity		
mystery		
the maw		
linking and joining		
pedestrian ways		
continuity		
hazards		

LINE	HEIGHT	COMPLEMENTARY	TRADITIONAL
COLOUR	WIDTH	VARIED	RESTORED
TEXTURE	DEPTH	HARMONIOUS	RECONSTRUCTED
SHAPE	PROJECTION	SENSITIVE	MODIFIED
MASS	RECESSION	AWKWARD	ADAPTED
VOLUME	PROGRESSION	CONVINCING	RESTRICTED
SPACE	MANIPULATION	COMFORTABLE	VARIED
CONTRAST	ENRICHMENT	ENHANCING	SIMILAR
PATTERN	DECORATION	OSTENTATIOUS	HIDDEN
RHYTHM	ACCENT	THOUGHTFUL	RESTRAINED
BALANCE	ARTICULATION	STIMULATING	LOCAL
LIGHT	EXPANSION	SUBTLE	VERNACULAR
MOVEMENT	CONTRACTION	CLAUSTROPHOBIC	SIMPLE
TIME	ENCLOSURE	BLAND	UNDULATING
DIRECTION	DEFINITION	ORDINARY	VERTICAL
SCALE	BARRIER	ELEGANT	HORIZONTAL
PROPORTION	LEVEL	WEAK	STRAIGHT
BALANCE	ACCENT	PLEASANT	CURVED
IMBALANCE	DECORATION	DISCORDANT	INTIMATE
SYMMETRY	BORING	POWERFUL	OPEN
ASYMMETRY	INTERESTING	UNCONVINCING	EXPOSED
ILLUSION	EXCITING	MONOTONOUS	LIMITED
ALLUSION	VITAL	DECREPIT	REGULAR
VARIETY	DOMINANT	EXPLOITED	UNIFORM
CHARACTER	DESTRUCTIVE	RENOVATED	REPETITIVE
CONSISTENCY	INVITING	REHABILIATED	
IDENTITY	POSITIVE	CONTEMPORARY	
UNITY	THREATENED	MODERN	

round blunt
hard soft
tall short flat
curved smooth
rough light
heavy cold warm

new old
modern
traditional
renovated
repaired
decayed

colourful bitty
crooked tidy
neat squiggly
patterned tatty
balanced
crumbly

puzzles
holes
faces
animals
plants
geometry

cosy funny
friendly pretty
ugly sad nice
plain unusual
frightening boring
dangerous

make up some words

Notation

A number of methods for recording the visual experience of townscape have been devised by architects and environmental artists. Some are complicated and sophisticated. Nevertheless they suggest ways of devising townscape notation that students can use to record what they see in their urban surroundings.

Keith Wheeler's notation system, explained here, derives mainly from Gordon Cullen but it has been much modified to make it usable by pupils.

John McKean's approach is to encourage students to devise their own system and to see how effective it is in communicating and comparing it with others.

Using Wheeler's notation does not depend on having any previous architectural knowledge. The notation acts in the same way as morphological mapping by supplying a system of symbols for recording certain types of observation. It has been employed successfully with the age-range of 13–18, thus making it suitable for CSE,

O- and A-level candidates. It has been most effective in encouraging geography teachers to include some consideration of aesthetic and design qualities in urban studies courses. It is hoped that teachers will experiment with the notation and make it a better educational tool.

McKean uses his approach with first year students of architecture, in order to develop that sensitivity to the day-to-day environment which he finds they haven't acquired in the sixth form at school. As to presentation, his instructions are that they should present A1 sheets showing their experience of the route:

'Like a musical score or choreographic notation, this will symbolically represent the sensory experience of the route — the sight, smell, touch and sound. Just as photographs of a trumpeter's hands or ballet dancer's feet have no place in their respective "scores", and words are used very sparingly, so you may not use photographs and words should be nearly redundant. But supplementary sheets with the materials study, with sketches and other observed data may be added.'

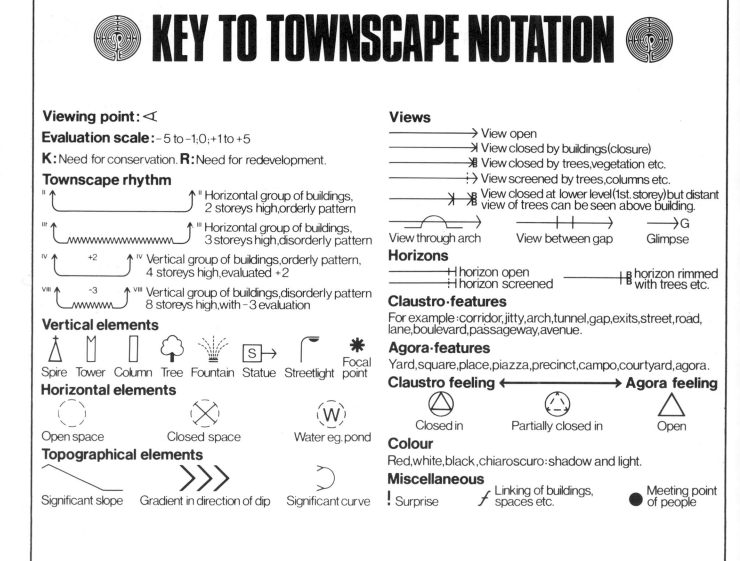

Slightly adapted, the approach could be used with many different age groups.

Brief

Select a route for study:

— The dynamics of the route: the route as you move along it; spaces which lead you, stop you, baffle you, open before you, enclose you. Views, vistas and landmarks; places to linger, places to move past fast.
— The cycles of the route: how does it (the objects, vegetation, spaces between them) change with the hours (as shadows move), with the days and with the seasons. (Visualize it very slippery with damp autumn leaves, icy winter wind, sunny long evening shadows, dusty windless heatwave, under full summer foliage, under a foot of dry snow.)
— And the cycles of its use: observe how it is peopled through 24 hours, through the 7 day cycle; visualize it in the different seasonal climates.

— The fabric along the route: the quality of architectural detail and street furniture, of colour, materials, richness of visual impression, scale, textures, reflectance, dullness, monotony, excitement.
— The effects of agents on this fabric of streetscape surfaces: ageing and weathering under the action of freezing, dust, chemicals, dirt, water, vegetation.
— The user of the route: assume possible roles — wheelchair-bound, a pair of 5 year-old friends with a ball, blind pedestrian with or without dog, mother with shopping and a 1 year-old in push chair. Assume modes of movement — feet, car driver, skateboard, bus conductor, bicycle, car and bus passenger. What are the key clues, what are the hazards; how does the perception of the space change for the latter group (who could all be the same person).

Now analyse why you chose the route which you did. Compare and contrast it with one other route.

TOWNSCAPE NOTATION OF A PART OF OADBY SHOPPING CENTRE

Instructions

Name.. Date.................
Class·Group...................................... Time.................
Weather description...

1
View from A
2
View from B to A
3
View from C to Council Offices
4
Houses between Brooksby Drive and Church Street
5
View from C to Church, showing schoolchildren 'notating'

Not to scale

NAME _____ SCHOOL _____

STUDY AREA _____ DATE _____

STUDY BRIEF   Ring the spaces which best describe your study area

                          (based on Walk Questionnaire: David Lowenthal 1972)

A	natural	–	–	–	–	–	artificial
B	contrast	–	–	–	–	–	uniform
C	people	–	–	–	–	–	things
D	ugly	–	–	–	–	–	beautiful
E	smelly	–	–	–	–	–	fresh
F	vertical	–	–	–	–	–	horizontal
G	ordered	–	–	–	–	–	chaotic
H	moving	–	–	–	–	–	motionless
I	smooth	–	–	–	–	–	rough
J	poor	–	–	–	–	–	rich
K	open	–	–	–	–	–	closed in
L	boring	–	–	–	–	–	interesting
M	old	–	–	–	–	–	new
N	quiet	–	–	–	–	–	noisy
O	vivid	–	–	–	–	–	drab
P	pleasant	–	–	–	–	–	unpleasant
Q	business use	–	–	–	–	–	living in
R	clean	–	–	–	–	–	dirty
S	full	–	–	–	–	–	empty
T	rural	–	–	–	–	–	urban
U	near views	–	–	–	–	–	far views
V	like	–	–	–	–	–	dislike
W	dark	–	–	–	–	–	light

add some of your own words ...

X	– – – – –
Y	– – – – –
Z	– – – – –

What do you like best about this site? _____

_____

What do you like the least? _____

_____

Any ideas for improvement? _____

_____

Art and the Built Environment © Schools Council

9 Critical skills: analysis, synthesis and evaluation

The essence of critical skill is to be able to understand the basis on which one's personal judgements are made and then to be prepared to explain them to other people.

The whole thrust of the exercises in this section is to help us reflect on our experience of townscape, to clarify our thinking about it and to use it as a basis for judgement. Attention must be given in preparing study methods of this kind to the values they imply and the kind of thinking they encourage. Conflict may arise here between teachers and pupils, for their previous experience and value systems are often very different. This means calling into question assumptions and previously held views which may be changed and modified by group experience and interaction. This will apply to teachers as well as pupils. Generally, being obliged to explain our view and opinions to others helps clarify our own thinking. It should not be worrying that there are disagreements so long as everyone is prepared to offer explanation or justification for their judgements.

Characteristically, study methods in this area will involve a combination of analysis, synthesis, evaluation and explanation, although the emphasis will vary.

Place assessment

This is another study method using vocabulary which can stimulate pupils to assess their feelings and reactions to the environment. It can be used to give some clues to the basic 'feel' of a place. Much simplified, it is a method derived from a fascinating research publication dealing with the comparative environmental assessment of four American cities by David Lowenthal and Marghita Riel. Instructions for using the place assessment sheet are shown on the sheet. It is a convenient way for pupils to compare first impressions quickly.

Townscape assessment — 'streetometer'

One of the most useful sets of material to emerge in recent years has been the informal packages produced under Eric Midwinter's supervision for the *Priority* programme in Liverpool. Of these, the 'streetometer' has achieved some fame, while 'leisure-measure', the 'serioscope', 'schoolscanner' and 'home rule' have been reproduced for local use only. The aim of the 'streetometer' was to provide a simple measure of the quality of individual streets, a measure which could be compared with others in the local area, or town-wide.

The 'streetometer' actually provides detailed comments on each variable employed. When each street has been examined against the 10 variables a score out of 100 is allocated. Like many simple and effective classroom activities, the 'streetometer' raises as many questions as it answers. A street scoring 100 could be a pretty unhappy place to live in with no visual stimuli of 'life'. What is the appropriate level of public advertising for a given situation? Who measures building conditions, what are their criteria and underlying aims in carrying out the assessment?

The authors of the 'streetometer' were the first to point out, however, that their idea was an example for adaptation in the classroom. For the senior student the issues raised in the design of this type of score sheet are likely to be as important as any fieldwork that is done with it.

streetometer

1	LITTER – excessive litter (0) grading to clean as a whistle (10)	
2	FLOORSCAPE – unmade, rutted, cracked paving (0) to new, decorative and easily negotiated paving (10)	
3	ADVERTISEMENTS – heavily plastered (0) to empty (10)	
4	CAR PARKING – crammed with cars (0) to empty (10)	
5	WIRESCAPE – sky view criss-crossed with wires and aerials (0) to clear (10)	
6	LANDSCAPE – devoid of vegetation (0) to luxuriant growths (10)	
7	BUILDING CONDITIONS – much dereliction (0) to perfect (10)	
8	ROAD SAFETY – measured in car frequency, visibility and protection for pedestrians	
9	AIR FRESHNESS – measured in terms of sensed smoke and smell	
10	NOISE NUISANCE – again measured aurally	

BUILDING IMPACT SCORE SHEET

Name of streetworker ------------------------------------

Group --

Date ---

Name of building

Assess each building against each criteria and score from 0 (awful) to 10 (excellent)

1	2	3	4	5	6	7	8	9	10

Criteria

Impact of building on the street

Size and scale

Relationship of building to surroundings

Choice of materials, textures, colours used

Standard of design of details

Value of external space made by building

Your possible enjoyment of living or working here

Satisfactory use of possibilities of site

General appearance of building as a whole

How well is it standing up to the effects of weather

Totals

Building location

1	
2	
3	
4	
5	
6	
7	
8	
9	
10	

Total score

Building appraisal — score sheet

Like other forms of notation and assessment this building impact score sheet devised by Keith Wheeler is only useful if it is used as a basis for discussion during which different points of view will emerge.

Building appraisal — CRIG

Based on his experience of working with architecture students and professional and lay people involved in local planning, Jeff Bishop prepared a building appraisal scheme derived from the work of Professor Ivor Smith which has been used by the Project. Jeff Bishop's approach derives from architecture but it offers scope for use in general education and emphasizes the contribution which the art teacher can make to the development of critical skills. The most effective way of recording the necessary information is through sketches, photographs, models, diagrams and maps. The study method depends on asking and answering a number of questions about CONTEXT, ROUTES, INTERFACE and GROUPING.

CRIG can be used in at least 3 ways. Students may be asked:

1   To appraise what is already built — from housing projects and factories to their own school.
2   To assess proposals — i.e. schemes submitted for planning application.
3   To contribute at the design stage — by understanding and being able to comment on architects' drawings.

Context

- What is the general pattern of the surrounding area; is it streets, squares, crescents, winding roads with set back development, etc?
- Scale of development; size of plots, shape, height and bulk of buildings, height/width ratio of streets, etc?
- Form of building in the area; consistent, varied, are basic style, materials used, details of windows, doors, etc?
- How do the public and private areas relate; houses on back of pavement, raised ground floor, blank walls, large front gardens, etc?
- What are the land uses in the area and in those immediately adjoining?
- Topography of the site; slopes, contours, views in and out? Environmental factors; orientation, exposure to wind and rain, humidity, daylight?
- Existing vegetation; grass, trees, shrubs, hedgerows?
- HOW DOES THE BUILDING RESPOND TO EACH AND ALL OF THESE?

Routes

- What are the routes currently used by pedestrians, cars, lorries, bicycles, motorcycles, prams, wheelchairs, visitors, children, service deliveries?
- What are desire lines?
- What are the flow patterns; are there peaks, troughs, regular movement, all one way, etc?
- Where are the 'nodes', the meeting points, and what, if anything happens there?
- What are the major generators of movement?
- HOW DOES THE BUILDING RESPOND TO EACH AND ALL OF THESE?
- What are the routes used within and around the building for all the groups described above? (Apply all the above questions again.)
- Does the route system make sense, is it coherent and convenient?
- Are the routes easily understood, especially for visitors, newcomers, servicing?
- Are the various parts of the building properly disposed to make the routes easy and clear?
- HOW EFFECTIVELY DO THE ROUTES WITHIN THE BUILDING WORK?

Interface

- Are the connections between the inside and the outside of the building clear?
- How are these connections made?
- Where inside joins outside is there an easy threshold?
- Are the various openings related to the planning inside, the view, the light, the degree of privacy needed, the location in the whole building etc.?
- Do the details of the building respond to the context and to the general layout of the building?
- Is there a well-controlled and clearly understandable hierarchy of public and private spaces? (This applies to both outside *and* inside.)
- Does the structure chosen for the building successfully control the effects of the climate — wind, rain, cold, sun, etc.?
- Is there scope for the users/occupants to make their own changes and 'personalize' the building?

Grouping

- Is the building sub-divided into different sections either by form or by details?
- Do these sub-divisions relate clearly to functions, social groups or aspects of the surrounding area?
- Is it clear what the various sub-divisions mean to people, e.g. is one section obviously a canteen or a gym?
- Are the various parts of the building planned carefully in relation to one another and to the site?
- Does the detail of the building respond to and reinforce the selected groupings?
- Is there enough relationship between the various parts for it to appear like one building, but enough variation to provide interest?
- Is it possible for other social groupings to occur in the building successfully?

CRIG

Context

general pattern of surrounding area?
scale of development?
form of building?
building in relation to site?
building in relation to natural elements?

Routes

what routes are there for different users?
are these the same as the desired routes?
where do people congregate? Where are the
'dead' spaces? Is the route system clear?
What are the major functions of the
route system?

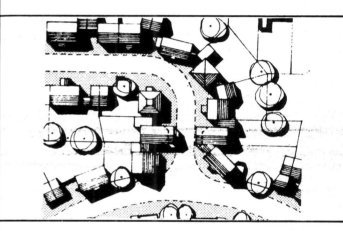

Interface

how does the interior relate to the
exterior of the building?
are spaces (public/private) clearly
defined?
does the building successfully adapt and
control the effects of climate?
is there scope for users or occupiers to
affect the building?

Grouping

how is the building made up?
does each part of the building
successfully relate to other parts?
how does the front of the building compare
with other sides?
how does the building rate in terms of
variety/cohesion/uniformity of elements?

CRIG in action: 2 worked examples

The following examples show how the CRIG factors could be applied in appraising buildings. This should provide a guide for how students might do their own appraisals. It reflects a personal interpretation by Jeff Bishop who uses a 7 point scale to categorize his assessment. A few comments should be made here about the examples.

The first example is built and is an office development in Bristol known as National Westminster Court ('Nat West Court'). If one thinks of the usual simple tower style of commercial development one can immediately see that Nat West Court is remarkable. It is clearly related to its Context and to its Routes, producing a lively grouping arrangement. This design was largely the result of pressure from a young planning officer who unfortunately died before the scheme was finished, but it shows the benefits of positive planning. What also makes the building fascinating for this exercise, however, is that on the Interface factor the building is rather poor. If the materials and details had been used on a simple tower block it would be very dull indeed, but because the building 'fits' so well on its site, one ceases to worry very much about the detail. This then illustrates the point made earlier that one does not always have to have a balance between all the CRIG factors; one can be less important than the others.

The second example was chosen for 3 reasons. First, it is a school, and although it is a primary school it shows that the factors can be applied to your own buildings as well. Secondly, it is not built and therefore gives an example of the appraisal of proposed buildings; (this example was 'passed' and has just started building). Thirdly, it provides a contrast with the first example because on this occasion the balance of factors was very different. Schools are (probably quite rightly) more about internal organization than about external image, whereas office blocks are very much public images of commercial companies. The school therefore gives little to, and takes little from, its Context; it relates well enough to Routes, and its Grouping is clear and ordered. In terms of Interface there is little doubt that it is better in this aspect than most schools.

On Broad Street the new building makes a very small effect, despite the fact that the two old shops are also part of the new development (they were rehabilitated). The new section repeats the frontage width of older development.

1 National Westminster Court

Context

The site is on the edge of the old city of Bristol and hence links with the very new and 'modern' areas to the west, of tower blocks on a podium, with raised walkways. The new building responds to this by having a small-scale side to the east and a larger block to the west.

The old city pattern is of narrow, tall, often winding streets with buildings set right up to the pavement. Plots are generally thin and small. Nat West Court repeats this very effectively in its eastern side with smaller blocks and tall spaces.

The old city wall creates a strong boundary and the new building reinforces this very strongly when it must have been very tempting to 'pretty' that side up.

Surrounding uses are mixed — churches, pubs, employment exchange, shops, offices, etc. Nat West Court is not all one office (there is a small separate suite), two old shops were improved rather than demolished, the pub was left and a new shop fitted in. The historical importance of the old 'Everards' facade is significant. There was a famous printing firm here and the facade is a superb example of Art Nouveau decoration. The facade is retained and used as the entrance. Some older areas are in the form of 'chambers' — backland courtyards reached by small alleys; Nat West Court has one of these.

The site was (when cleared) *flat, featureless and without vegetation.* John's Court (along John Street) has a few trees and shrubs. There were no *views* out of the site except by building upwards and although the main block is not very high it provides views out. From a distance even the main block has little effect on the skyline of the old city. The old alleys, etc., provided very good protection from *wind and rain* at the expense of a degree of overshadowing. The wind and rain protection is still good, but there is now more light getting in.

Assessment:

Good	1	2	3	4	5	6	7	Bad
	X							

Diagram showing the site in its context.

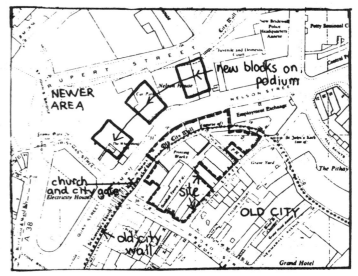

The old road is successfully retained, while being closed to through traffic and widened to create a place for people to linger.

Routes

The only *main vehicle route* is Nelson Street on the north-west edge of the site. There is some vehicle movement along John Street for servicing and along Broad Street. The scheme responds to these adequately by taking the car parking off Nelson Street at a lower level than the main floors (and hence reinforcing the 'city wall' idea!). John Street has been closed to through traffic and is now used

Map showing the major movement lines around the site

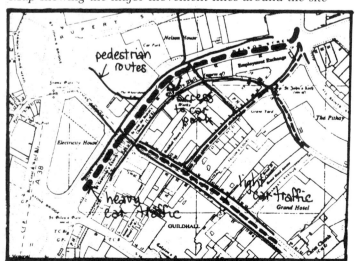

much more by pedestrians. Broad Street remains an access/service road because the building shows little on that side. There are several pedestrian routes through alleys and along flanking roads. The new podium system will shortly be finished but until then there is an abrupt stop along Nelson Street with a change of level. The alley routes are all retained and even enhanced — especially in the courtyard by the pub, used as a meeting area. Little John Street (between John Street and Nelson Street) has been closed and is now a pedestrian route which will link with a bridge across to the podium. The small shop is very effectively placed near this bridge.

The old layout of the city was *easily comprehensible* because it was an irregular grid. The newer area is rather confusing because the blocks on the podium always seem to be in the way. Nat West Court sensibly relates to the former system while nevertheless linking to the latter.

The *entrances* to the building are mixed. The 'Everards' entrance is a very good use of an old building and is in the right place. The other entrance is rather hidden away, but (1) it is only really for the office workers and (2) it will seem better when the podium bridge is built and more people walk by.

The internal organization is very complex and difficult to learn. It is, however, an office and not a public building; therefore, most users are 'regulars'.

Assessment:

Good	1	2	3	4	5	6	7	Bad
	X							

Interface

There are many different styles of building in the surrounding area. Older ones use brick or stone with vertical windows in walls. Ground floors are often different from the others, floor heights are varied and there is a lot of intricate detail. Newer buildings are frame construction with mostly concrete or brick panels between. All the floor heights are the same and there is much less detail.

The building responds to these things in some ways. The materials are mainly brick and concrete in what could be a frame construction but not necessarily (in fact it is a frame). The brick has no strong precedent in the area. The ground floor is the same, and there is a rather half-hearted attempt at a parapet. The details do, however, change a little, with arches, bays, balconies, larger windows, etc., in certain relevant places.

The 'Everards' entrance is, surprisingly, very good for the image of Nat West and in the sunken courtyard there is even a little brick version of the Nat West symbol. The holes in the walls for windows suggest individual offices, but they are in fact mostly large open areas. The 'ownership' of the area by the pub is clear: it is public. The undercover route (along Little John Street) feels almost private because the route to the bridge is not yet open, and the sunken courtyard is clearly very private although anyone can look into it.

There are a few minor status symbols to be noticed (balconies for some individual offices) but there is little opportunity for occupants to personalize either inside or outside.

These examples show the limited variation in detail — panels below windows, balconies, materials, etc. Despite this the changes have an effect in making different parts of the building look different.

Assessment:

Good	1	2	3	4	5	6	7	Bad
					X			

Grouping

The two different sides of the site demand different responses and they get them. The east side is more small-scale, and the west includes the only high bit. Because of a wish to tie heights into surrounding buildings to respect the old routes, the very varied, complex and interesting form responds well to this.

It is difficult to think of Nat West Court as *one* building. It can never all be seen (or even guessed at) at once and is therefore more a group of buildings. The one separately rented office is clearly detached from the others and the three old shop/office units are kept as they were before, enhancing their uniqueness and yet relating to the group.

Because this building responds to the external constraints to make its groupings, these groups do not relate to the internal organization of the building. The planning is nearly all open office areas with some individual rooms, toilets, etc. The canteens and some offices are expressed differently on the outside.

Assessment:

Good	1	2	3	4	5	6	7	Bad
			X					

Conclusions

An average of the assessments would suggest a score of 2.75 but I would not hesitate to put it, overall clear in

Like	1	2	3	4	5	6	7	Dislike
		X						

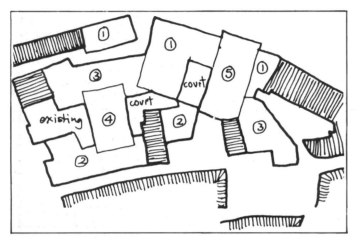

This plan shows surrounding buildings and those excluded from the scheme as

The heights are shown by the numbers:
1 is 2 storeys above the podium
2 is 3 storeys above the podium
3 is 5 storeys above the podium
4 is 6 storeys above the podium
5 is 8 storeys above the podium

This photograph of the model shows the complexity of the Grouping in Nat West Court. There are many blocks of different heights and the shape is impossible to conceive of in terms of being a pedestrian.

2 St John's School

Context

The site is in the high part of Clifton, a major Georgian/Regency/Victorian residential suburb of Bristol, and slopes down to the south. This part of Clifton is more mixed than some parts and the site itself links an area of mainly semi-detached villas to an area of mostly tight and small terraces.

Worrall Road has lost its other side and no longer feels like a two-sided street but the demolition has opened up major views across Bristol, to the south.

Mornington Road is a narrow cobbled lane with high walls, but is surprisingly well used.

Anglesea Place was a narrow, tall street which again has lost one side. The only major building on the site now is the existing Junior School which creates a high, dramatic corner and contains a fascinating series of rooms inside. (It will be demolished.)

Surrounding uses are mixed although mainly residential. There are shops, pubs, small industries and two clubs. The site has few major features except the big drop from Worrall Road. There are some old garden walls, shrubs and small trees.

The new school building responds to some of these features. It flanks Worrall Road and so partially recreates a second side to the street. It does not really do more than this and leaves a big (and probably inevitable) blank along Anglesea Place. Given the problems, some good attempts have been made to use what is on the site. The drop from

This shows Worrall Road, the irregular terrace, the narrow street, and the traffic.

Worrall Road is used to hide the bulk of the hall; the old garden walls, shrubs, etc., are used to create different areas in the playground and the high walls along Mornington Road are improved and gaps filled in. The school makes good use of the southerly aspect and views.

Assessment:

Good	1	2	3	4	5	6	7	Bad
				X				

(which is very good considering the problems of a rather lumpy building on a large site.)

This map shows the site and its surroundings, including the nearby shopping area of Whiteladies Road.

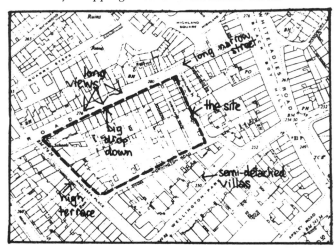

Routes

Worrall Road is a minor short-cut attracting *through traffic,* but Anglesea Place and Mornington Road are very quiet. (Vehicular traffic is surprisingly relevant to this school because it is C of E and hence has no catchment area — children come from long distances, often in cars). Worrall Road is used a little for *parking by shoppers* going to a major shopping street at the end — Whiteladies Road — and there is a very little off-street parking for local residents. The pavements are narrow.

The major approaches to the site for *pedestrians* are along Worrall Road from the east, less from the west, up Anglesea Place and perhaps a very small amount from Mornington Road, sneaking along from the southeast. The building can do little to ease vehicular traffic problems but provides a car park for staff. The pavement along Worrall Road will be widened to ease congestion and hopefully prevent accidents. It would seem that the children will probably either enter the school from Worrall Road or at the southeast corner, crossing the playground — the problem is that the latter entry place will depend on how staff and caretaker manage the playground.

Within the building the circulation is basically very simple. From Worrall Road (for parents and others) the staff area is immediately accessible. For children they go either straight down or along and down through the half-level section to the east.

It is probably for reasons of economy or fire safety, but the main staircase appears very minor and rather tucked away instead of making a positive and interesting link between the two main levels. It is also a pity that when one comes in off Worrall Road there is no clear view through across Brisol.

Assessment:

Good	1	2	3	4	5	6	7	Bad
			X					

Interface

The set-back of the wall along Worrall Road begins to indicate an entrance and the simple end to the wall makes the entrance fairly clear. This main entrance and some of the others are under cover which helps to provide a breathing-space between outside and inside.

The windows are mostly small (for energy-saving reasons?) but clearly indicate the location of the rather inward-looking class spaces. Other windows are just large glazed panels indicating resource areas. The inward-looking nature of the classes is helped by the circulation/resource areas: the latter are clearly general, semi-public spaces not 'owned' by any one class.

The structure is clear and straightforward and is consistent with the size and use of the various spaces. Overhangs, small windows, covered areas and rooflights show careful thought about controlling the climate. The

Plan showing main approaches to site and entrances to school. Vehicles all enter at southwest corner.

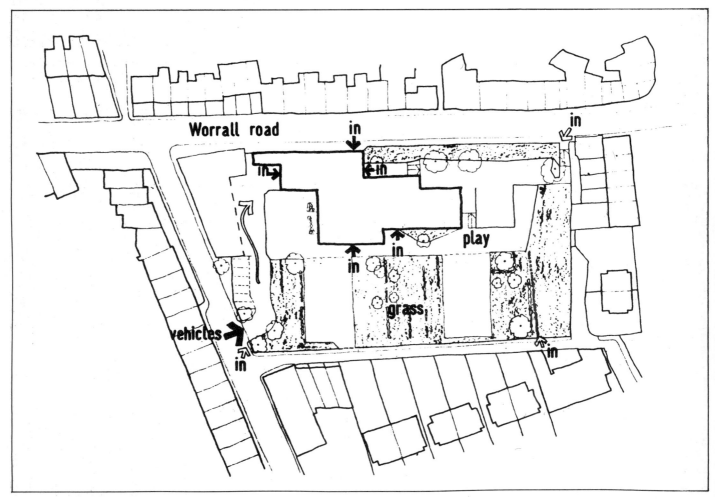

materials are acceptable for the area but a lot will depend on the actual colours and textures. Inside the school there is a lot of scope for staff and children to use and adapt the building, to make it their own.

Assessment:

Good	1	2	3	4	5	6	7	Bad
			X					

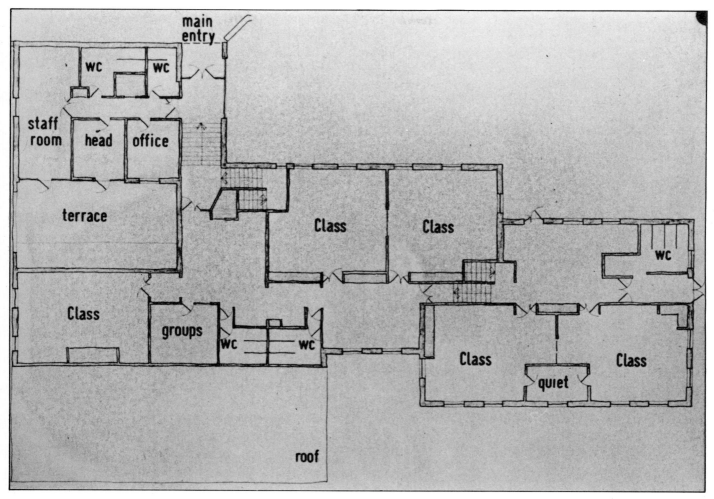

Upper level plan showing main entrance and main routes through, including tight stair down to lower levels. N.B. — two classes at right are half-level down.

The section shows clearly the clever use of the steep drop from Worrall Road to hide the hall and provoke the long low roof.

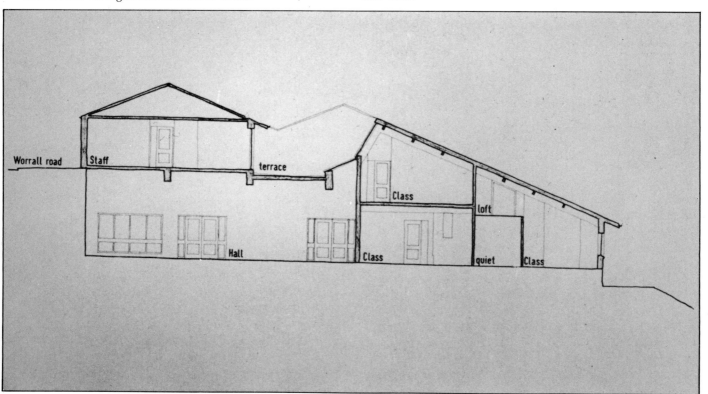

The position of the school on a sloping site set back from Worrall Road is shown. The building is seen not as one large mass but as a series of interconnecting units.

Grouping

The bulk of the building is very well broken down into clear and obvious parts without being bitty like many new schools. The divisions clearly relate to what is happening within the building and are not inconsistent with the surroundings. The steep drop from Worrall Road has been used very effectively to hide the often obtrusive bulk of the main hall. The staff area is nicely detached, related to Worrall Road, and yet is still part of the overall building. The plan avoids the ambitious arrangement of small teaching areas merging into large resource areas by giving clear but not rigid definition to each class space. Various forms of teaching could be used. Children group together in schools in a variety of different ways and the building does provide lots of different sorts of places for these groups. The detail of the building seems to respond to the various sub-divisions.

Assessment:

Good	1	2	3	4	5	6	7	Bad
		X						

Conclusions

An average of the 4 assessments would place the building exactly in No 3, but in relation to other school designs it is better than that — its failures are the problems of all school buildings and are perhaps insoluble. So:

Like	1	2	3	4	5	6	7	Dislike
		X						

Building appraisal for 16–19 year olds using CRIG

Jeff Bishop has worked out carefully the scope offered to the teacher by CRIG:

Having set my own 'context' for the subject of building appraisal, it now remains to suggest a series of exercises through which the concepts can be taught.

I have in fact described briefly the 3 main aspects to be taught: appraisal of buildings already built, appraisals of proposals, and contributions at the design stage (see next Chapter). Before embarking on these in detail, however, one point needs to be made about the work in terms of communication. Architecture depends very heavily on the use of drawing techniques, many of which are formalized into a 'language' inadequately understood by the layman. Plans, sections, certain 3-dimensional projections and even some types of sketch or diagram need to be studied before really fruitful communication can occur between architects and the public. The techniques are not difficult to understand but merely need experience. Apart from looking at books and slides of drawings and buildings the only specific suggestion I can make for developing an understanding quickly is that teachers get hold of a set of drawings of their own school. These always exist for new schools and for a remarkable number of old schools — even if they are in a cardboard tube in the archives. The benefits of looking at the school are firstly that you do not need to go on a journey to study it, and secondly and more important, you can directly experience the building while studying its drawings. In general, however, the problem is an example of 'chicken and egg' so the exercises themselves can be regarded as a way of

developing an ability to read drawings, and a high level of expertise is therefore certainly not an essential prerequisite.

Introduction

Immediately one is faced with a further example of 'chicken and egg' because it is highly likely that the concepts introduced here — CRIG — are unfamiliar to the teacher as well as the students! What is needed, however, is an opening session when the CRIG factors are introduced to the students using 3 resources:

1   The illustrations and examples given in this section.
2   Examples known to the teacher, probably a random. collection of illustrations.
3   Examples from the local area, familiar to both teacher and students — (especially valuable because they may know more about context than you!).

The teacher can and actually *should* develop the list of questions on each factor to respond to particular local factors (e.g. climate, materials) and to specific building types ('status' steps to the town hall, etc.).

Appraising what is built

The 'what' in this case may be any building or a group such as a housing scheme or school campus. I have used mostly newish buildings because my own slide library consists mainly of examples of these, but old buildings can make a fascinating contrast and the choice should be related both to the availability and accessibility of examples in the area and to the examples used in other parts of the art curriculum. Certainly there is no need to think only of 'great' examples; almost any building will suffice. Thought should be given to the selection of buildings which one can enter and even explore; this is why one's own school is so useful, (even in winter when little other environmental work can be done). Finally I would personally argue for the use of more than one building because of the benefits of comparison. There may be 2 or 3 and although it would be ideal to use, for example, 2 small housing schemes showing different approaches, almost any comparison can be used successfully.

Having selected what to appraise, the next step is to prepare for the visit by looking again at the list of factors and asking oneself whether any other questions are relevant to the particular buildings to be studied. Then one is ready to go out.

Each student should be asked to prepare an appraisal using each of the CRIG factors, and this can be presented through sketches, photographs, diagrams, maps and even quick models, supported by written comment. The two examples given in this chapter should help. The appraisal is not just a written analysis, however. It demands some expression of opinion. These examples show the use of a 7 point scale at the end of each of the 4 sections with a rating given for the buildings. This should be done but then there is one further task. Remember my earlier comments that all I am proposing here is a way of finding common ground on some aspects — not all. It is also important therefore to ask for a final assessment in terms of like and dislike. It is absolutely essential that students learn that even though they may ultimately not like a building very much, it can nevertheless answer satisfactorily most of the questions in the CRIG factors. One has to be prepared, in many areas of life and not just architecture, to accept different people's perceptions and values — provided that the common ground is adequately covered. The like and dislike scale can be a 7 point scale, as with the others.

Depending on the size of the group it is possible to provide a quick summary of the assessments of each building under each factor, and on like/dislike, by simply counting up the ticks in each column and seeing which column scores highest, which scores lowest, etc.

Appraising proposals

The explanation of this section can be fairly short because much of what I have just said applies equally to this exercise.

The 'proposals' are designs submitted by architects (or developers, builders, etc.) for planning permission. In every local planning office there is a 'development control'

section which vets applications and it is part of the planning law of this country that all applications should be open to public inspection — even the authority's own work.

You could probably arrive at the planning office one day and request access to current planning applications — and be successful. Some degree of further preparation would, however, at least mean you might be successful more than once!

First, you should contact the person in charge of development control — this could be the Chief Planning Officer in small districts — and talk about what you would like to do. Secondly, you should keep up to date with the applications passing through — local papers or published lists will help here — and thirdly, you should make an appointment giving as much notice as possible.

There is in fact a more important reason for contacting the planning department. Apart from looking at and appraising proposals (as in my second example earlier) it would add considerably to the experience if you could see the officers' report to the planning committee and then observe what happens to the application when it gets to the planning committee. You *should* be able to see the reports after the council meeting if not before and obviously the ideal way of observing the fate of the applications would be to attend the committee meeting — dates are available from the council and most meetings are now public.

This second exercise then has one basic and 2 optional components:

1   A *visit to the planning office* where the selected schemes are appraised exactly as described in the previous sections although photographs are not possible. Even if you are not able to use reports or attend councillors' meetings, one should be able to get an informal, personal, off-the-record comment from the development control officer and then, at the very least, discover whether the applications were passed or refused.
2   A *look at officers' reports* to compare their comments with the students' analyses. Remember that most applications raise many planning issues other than just the appearance of the building. If you are lucky (or unlucky) enough to live in an area where the planning department has produced design guides, these are usually well worth getting.
3   *Attendance at the planning committee meeting* or some idea from reports of what the committee decided. If you feel strongly that the councillors are being arbitrary, do not be afraid to show them your studies and argue the point with them.

CRIG adaptations

In the course of the project it was found effective to produce a number of worksheets based on CRIG. In some cases these were summaries of the main themes, in others they involved adapting the ideas to interiors. 3 examples are shown here.

study area ....

Observe the study area from a number of viewpoints,
considering the following questions:

CONTEXT
what is the PATTERN of the area?
what is the SCALE of the development?
what is the FORM of the buildings?
what kind of SITE is it?

ROUTES
what Routes are provided?
do PEOPLE use alternative routes?
are there any MEETING points?
are routes clearly DEFINED, easily UNDERSTOOD?
what kind of TRAFFIC circulation is there?

INTERFACE
does the exterior of the building explain its
interior function (or does it hide it?)
how does the inside CONNECT with the outside?
what clues define PUBLIC and PRIVATE space?

GROUPING
how is the BUILDING made up?
what MATERIALS, CONSTRUCTION METHODS
have been used? why?
how do all the parts of the building RELATE
to each other?

Record information through annotated drawings,
maps, diagrams.
Use these to make a critical appraisal of the building
and give reasons for your judgements.

Art and the Built Environment © Schools Council

townscape assessment

STUDY BRIEF

Select a suitable study area - for example part of a street, a cul de sac, a bus lay-by, a shopping parade - which will enable you to make a CRITICAL APPRAISAL of a group of buildings in relation to the space in which they stand.

PLAN

Make a plan of the layout of the site (Consider objects buildings spaces routes slope edges.)
Make up your own notation system for this.

DRAWINGS

Choose three viewpoints and make a series of drawings to explain what the study area looks like.

ANNOTATIONS

Label your drawings to provide as full a description as possible. Any information you cannot indicate clearly through drawing, indicate in words.

COMMENTS

Comment on the design qualities (or lack of them) stating your personal opinion. EXPLAIN your judgements. Consider how it might be improved.

building (interior) appraisal

study brief

make an initial exploration of the building. make a study of one particular space in greater detail.

MAP (first impressions)

Attempt to record your impressions of the building as you move through it. Record your route. Make notes of your feelings. Where you have a choice of route, note why you chose to go one way rather than another. Where did you stop? Why? What interested you?

DIAGRAM (layout/movement)

Draw a diagram of the layout of the building as you have understood it from your initial exploration. Explain movement and circulation patterns of which you were aware, and indicate what happens in the building.

ANNOTATED DRAWINGS (spaces)

Compare the design qualities of a number of the spaces you encountered. Which did you prefer? Why? How were they used?

DEVELOPMENT Evaluate your favourite space in terms of the following features (plus any others you consider relevant) – function · shape · size · light · colour · structure · building materials · sounds · services – lighting heating water ventilation – signs · objects · furniture · personalisation.

10 Design skills

Most design activity in schools is product-oriented and is conducted to reveal the nature of design. In the Project a rather different approach is taken. Here, designing is used simply as a study method. The activity, which emphasizes synthesis, is a good medium for understanding directly the whole range of environmental experiences and, because it looks to the future, encourages lively critical awareness. This is an aspect of the Project which offers scope for further development.

The house game

Here are the instructions for *The House Game*, devised by Jeff Bishop:

This game, or exercise, is remarkably simple to set up and operate and yet can be used at almost any level with people of any age — only the number of issues, the connections between them, the verbal skills and, perhaps, the sophistication of the results will change.

This set of instructions was mainly derived from doing the exercise with 9/10/11 year olds (as well as once with trainee teachers). It can be simplified or extended in many ways and some suggestions for extension are given at the end.

The main aim in devising it was to demonstrate to non-architects the number of factors which have to be juggled even in the simplest design problem, how any answer is almost always a personal one and that therefore there are no 'right' answers.

In more conventional school terms it can be used to develop thinking skills, language, ideas about the environment, empathy for others, working together, simple statistics (correlating results), etc. Perhaps the most important notion, however, is the one already mentioned — there is no right answer, it all depends on how *you* value certain aspects for *your* world. In this way the traditional dependency on teachers for 'the' answer is dispensed with and the beginnings are laid for the development of judgement.

Sequence of events

1   *Make the houses* — the master sheet illustrated can be copied to provide as many kits as you need. Each person or group needs 1 sheet i.e. 12 houses. First cut along the thickest black lines to make 12 long rectangles with nicks across near either end. Hold face up and fold down along the next thinnest lines (5 of these). As it begins to join up you can see how the two nicks can be slotted in and the flap folded under. No glueing is necessary and it should be obvious that you now have houses with back garden.

2   *Sites* — a piece of land is represented by a piece of A4 size paper. The size of paper is crucial but colour and thickness are not. You will also need glue.

3   *The task* — each person or group are then told that they have to get *all 12* houses on the site in as interesting, convenient and economic a layout as possible.

They have to do this in the light of the following basic list:

a *Sun* — must get to each garden. Identify a wall or window facing the sun or make a sun to put up. Point out that gardens do not have to face straight to it but roughly within 45 degrees (show this if necessary).

b *Footpath* — there must be at least a footpath to every house; no-one must be cut off.

c *Parking* — cars can be parked right by the houses (in which case roads must be shown) or in a group/groups around the edge. Assume roads can enter the site anywhere.

d *Open space* — there must be as large as possible an area(s) of open space, marked as such (write on in green pen). It does not all have to be in one piece.

4   *Time and finishing* — with most groups around 30 minutes has been plenty of time, but there is nothing crucial about any period. When a final idea is ready it can be stuck down, and roads, open space and parking marked on.

5   *Evaluation* — There is a simple evaluation form illustrated. Each individual or group is given one for their design or, if, time permits, one for everybody's. If each person has 1 form, the whole group look at each in turn and a count is made of who puts their vote in each box on the form. The leader simply asks 'How many people think it is *very* attractive' or 'How many people think it is *fairly* expensive' etc., etc? Doing it this way is quick and enjoyable but it is like any public ballot — votes are 'influenced'. If you choose to get everybody to fill in their own forms on each design, there is then a need for someone to count ticks in boxes and produce a summary, but it is fairer.

Obviously there is little a leader can say during the exercise to determine what is meant by 'attractive'. 'Convenient' is also difficult to judge, although broadly the simpler layouts are more convenient. Cheapness is, to some extent, easier. The most expensive layout is random detached houses, the next cheapest — ordered detached houses, and so on through semi-detached to short terraces at angles, to short parallel terraces, to the cheapest — long terraces.

Points to make, issues to raise

Within the first few minutes it will become obvious that the attractive layouts are the most expensive, that fairly attractive and cheap layouts are inconvenient, etc. Discussion then moves onto the relative merits of terraces (which give large areas of open space) as opposed to detached houses (which are expensive), as opposed to layouts which keep cars out (making deliveries difficult), etc.

Pushing houses together gets nice open space but cuts down sunlight (and privacy). Discussion can also move onto *who* one is designing for. Children may love to get to play space without crossing roads but parents have to walk

1

210 mm

297 mm

2

3

4

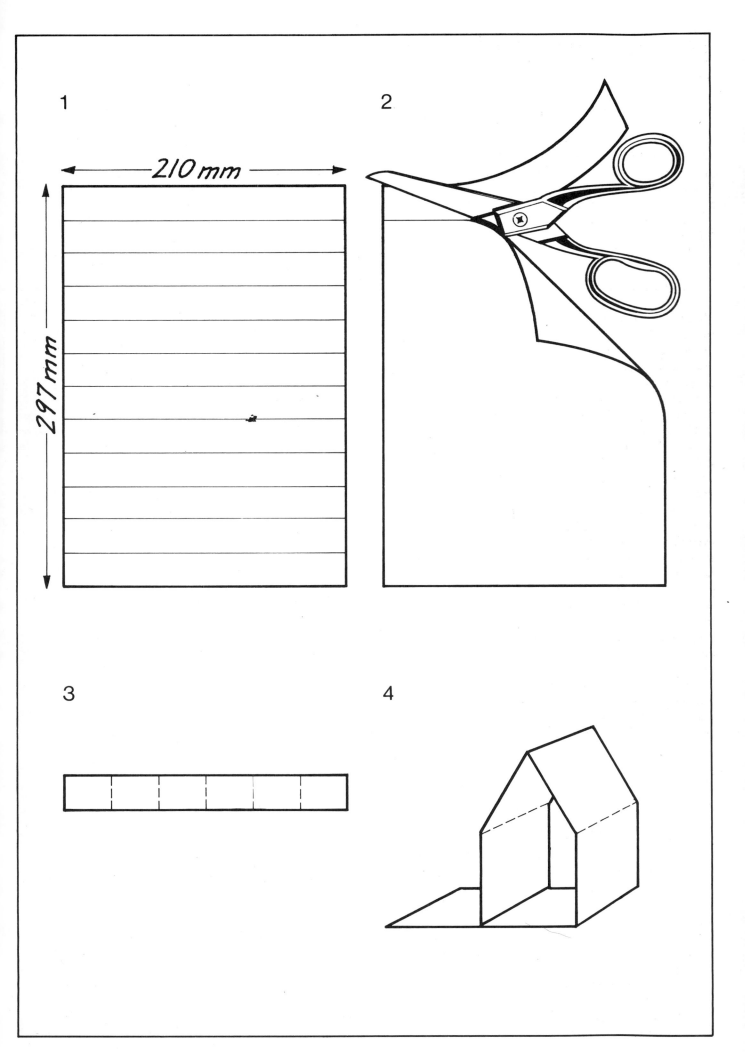

a long way from (probably) an insecure car park. Children may like large open spaces but parents do not like terrace houses (for noise, but they are good for cost). If cars come right up to the houses, all the road is open space lost.

Less directly, issues arise about density. If someone wants more land or less houses, what are the implications of this on a large scale — loss of countryside? If the process is very much about personal judgement then *who* decides; what right do architects, planners and councillors have to do this for *you*? Work can be prefaced by, or developed into, studies for housing; more statistical work can be done, geography can develop.

The list is almost endless but there are 3 basic sorts of addition:

1   More/different items to add to the list of parking, open space, etc. Examples are play space, shop or pub (fold garden under house), other buildings — choice by participant.

2   Other criteria to think about, e.g. if easy to find one's way around, good for deliveries (furniture, bread, milk, hearse!), easy for the postman, noise between houses, privacy, adaptable, etc.

3   Relate the abstract 'site' to a real site in your area by (a) fixing where the road comes in, and (b) describing the surroundings. Larger or smaller sites, tower blocks, bungalows, etc.

	Very	Fairly	In between	Fairly	Very	
Attractive						Unattractive
Convenient						Inconvenient
Economic						Expensive

Infill exercises

These exercises have been devised by Jeff Bishop as a possible development of CRIG (see Chapter 9). Here he describes what is involved:

'The examples illustrated are probably the best two one could use — a house and an office — but others are possible such as a shop with flats above, a garden, a Citizens Advice Bureau, etc. Again it is not essential to select major sites; a gap in a terrace or a parade of shops, a small corner site or a traffic island are all suitable sites, giving constraints and possibilities. The exercise is not to produce a solution but to compare various possible solutions to see how they satisfy each of the CRIG factors. It should be obvious on almost any site that no single solution will satisfy all the factors and one can make the point that all design is an endless series of balances between long lists of pros and cons.

Having identified the sites and decided what should happen to them, the students then study the surroundings (the Context) and include in this studies of the way surrounding buildings respond to that context — and to the Routes, the Interface and the Groupings. The students can produce from this photographs, sketches, maps, diagrams, models — all with the gap to be filled. They can then start to suggest ways of putting a house or an office on the site to respond to CRIG — each factor in turn, then perhaps all together. This can be done through sketches, etc.,

and photomontage is a very effective technique. They then comment, as in my examples, on each solution and again assess it on a scale for each factor. There can then be a class discussion of the relative merits of each idea.'

Infill — house

Page 80 shows 2 ways of exploring possible solutions to putting a new house/houses in a gap in a terrace. On the left are 3 alternatives on plan, each giving different pros and cons. On the right are 3 different facades — missing out the straight replica. For facades a photograph of the street is a good base on which to superimpose ideas.

Infill — commercial

The following examples illustrate some possible basic solutions to a corner site being used for commercial offices. The site can be assumed to be empty and the ideas illustrate a variety of approaches. The plans are put adjacent to drawings using a form of projection called axonometric. Although this sounds difficult it can soon be mastered and on page 83 you can see some of the basic tricks involved in such drawings. Obviously, street elevations (probably photographs) could be used instead and detailed facades produced, as with the house example. Each solution can be evaluated. The basic solutions are followed by more extreme examples.

INFILL - HOUSE

This sheet shows two ways of exploring possible solutions to putting a new house/ houses in a gap in a terrace. On the left are three alternatives on plan, each giving different pros and cons. On the right are three different facades - missing out the straight replica. For facades a photograph of the street is a good base on which to superimpose ideas.

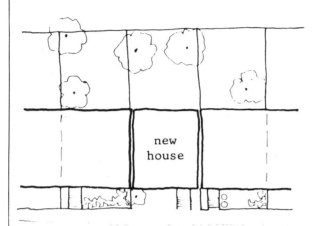

new house on same lines as existing, must relate closely

1960's compromise, floor levels unrelated, mixture of expressions, bitty.

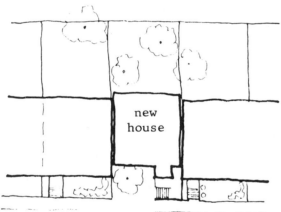

new house set back, not so essential to relate closely

1920s modern style, totally unrelated to adjacent houses, different scale, height etc.

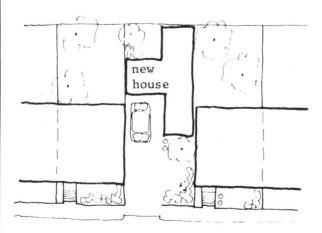

new single storey house sited at back of plot

1970's 'vernacular' style, fitting in but exaggerated, rather lumpy and clumsy

INFILL - COMMERCIAL

The following two sheets illustrate some possible basic solutions to a corner site being used for commercial offices. The site can be assumed to be empty and the ideas illustrate a variety of approaches. On this page plans are put adjacent to drawings using a form of projection called axonometric. Although this sounds difficult it can soon be mastered and the final sheet shows some of the basic tricks involved in such drawings. Obviously, street elevations (probably photographs) could be used instead and detailed facades produced as with the house example. Each solution can be evaluated. Overleaf is another sheet of more extreme examples.

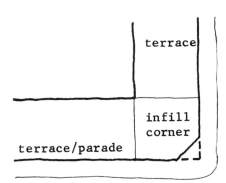
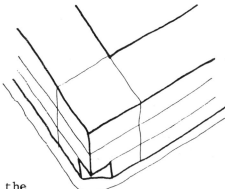

corner site with 3-storey block filling most of the corner. Lower storey angled to respond to pedestrian movement.

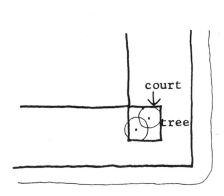
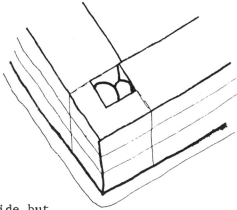

block which appears to be solid from the outside but which has an internal court allowing light and vegetation in.

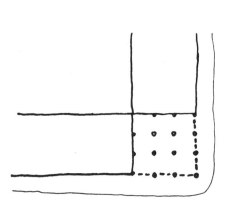
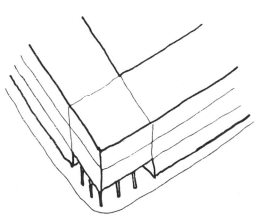

office block on two floors only above open arcade which can be used for sitting, meeting, exhibitions etc.

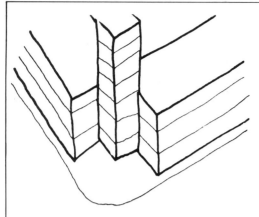

Putting the same volume into a
building twice as high

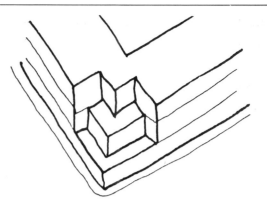

ziggurat form stepping back
giving roof terraces, lose space

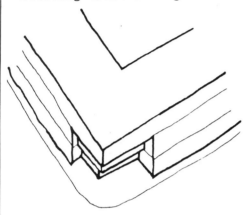

stepping outwards, providing protection
but cutting out light, lose space

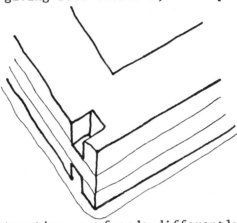

treating one facade differently to the
other, one fits in, the other stands
out (or rather back)

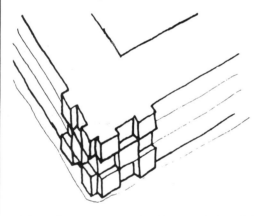

'lego' games with form of building, very
interesting, rather obtrusive and expensive

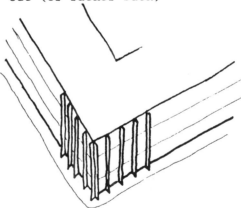

vertical emphasis, slit windows and
projecting fins.

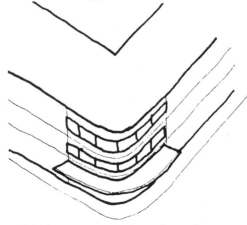

1930's International Modern style,
horizontal emphasis.

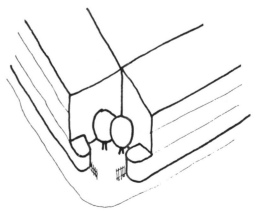

1970's ecology style, trees, grass and
goats.

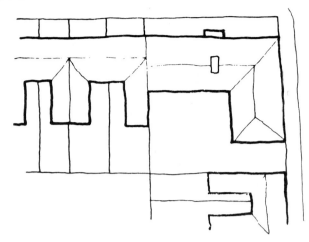

AXONOMETRICS - take the corner house shown in plan and elevation above

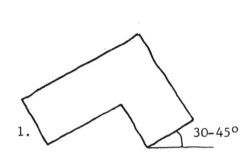

1.   30-45°

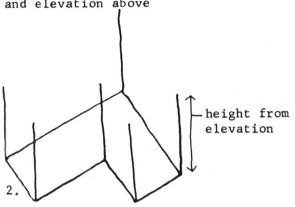

2.   height from
     elevation

First draw the plan at around 45° to the axis of the paper (1), then project up
the vertical lines of the corners to the actual scale height (2)

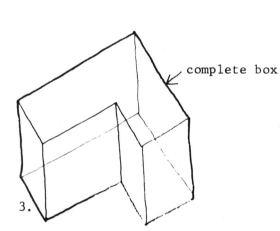

3.   complete box

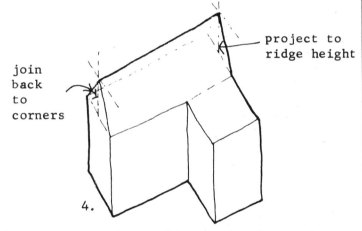

join
back
to
corners

project to
ridge height

4.

complete the basic box (3), then do the first part of the roof by projecting up to
the centre of the ridge (4), join the other roof section (5) and add detail (6).

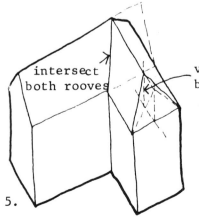

intersect
both rooves

vertical, set
back for hip roof

5.

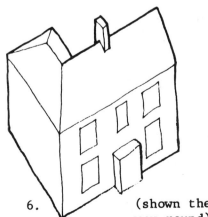

6.   (shown the other
     way round)

83

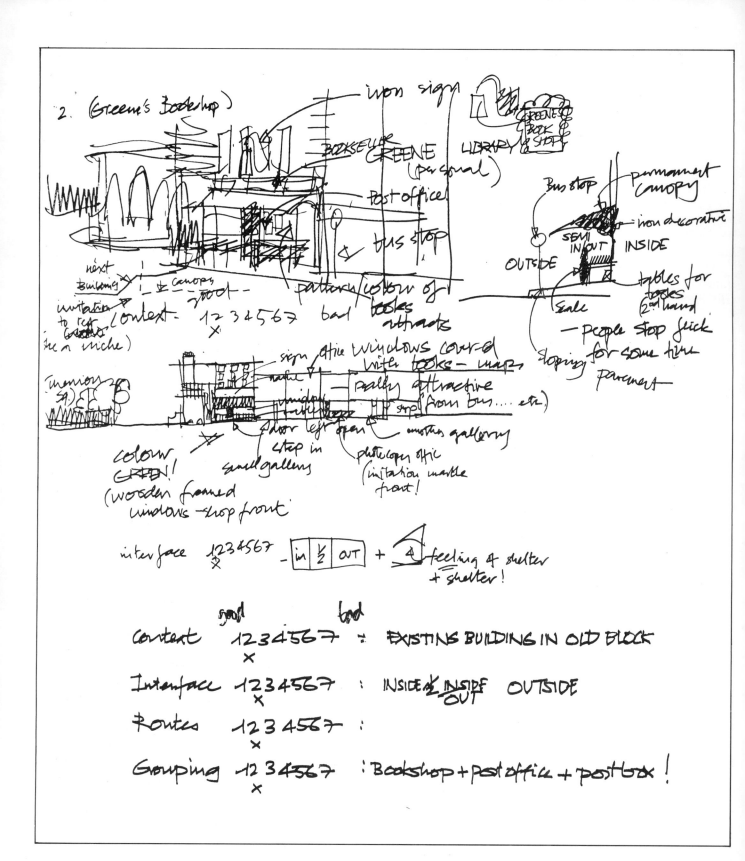

2. (Greene's Bookshop)

iron sign

GREENE'S BOOK SHOP

BOOKSELLER GREENE (personal) — LIBRARY

Post office

& bus stop

next building — canopy — roof

invitation to rest (context — 1234567 bad) tree in niche)

pattern/colour of books attracts

Bus stop — permanent canopy — iron decorative

SEMI IN/OUT   INSIDE

OUTSIDE   Scale   tables for books (2nd hand)

tables for sale

— people stop & look for some time

sloping pavement

(interior sq.)

sign attic windows covered with books — maps — really attractive stop (from bus .... etc)

door left open — another gallery

step in   small gallery   photocopier office (imitation marble front!)

colour GREEN! (wooden framed windows — shop front

interface 1234567 — [in | ½ | out] + feeling of shelter + shelter!

good   bad

Context   1234567 : EXISTING BUILDING IN OLD BLOCK
              x

Interface 1234567 : INSIDE INSIDE OUT OUTSIDE
              x

Routes   1234567 :
              x

Grouping   1234567 : Bookshop + post office + post box !
              x

11 Communication skills

An important aspect of ABE work is to have something to say about the environment and an effective way of saying it.

This is basic to much of art education in schools, where emphasis is placed on graphic communication, and we are very aware of the value of expressive media in providing a means of realizing a subjective, emotional response to place.

However, the Project has also been especially interested in the use of such media to develop discriminatory and critical skills, and has given particular attention to 2 areas: the use of drawing and photography.

Drawing

Drawing is particularly important for ABE work, as it permits an extended involvement with the environment, and imposes a particular rhythm and pace of working, which permits the observer to establish relationships not at first apparent. Drawing as a vehicle for eliciting a heightened response may be based on the fact that it encourages an emotional engagement more difficult to establish through more superficial approaches. Ralph Jeffery observes:

'drawing imposes a different rhythm on experience. Having drawn something, the thing you have drawn takes on values. If you draw something you have to look very hard at it. It is the making of judgements that the long-term process of drawing implies which seems to me to be of great value in increasing our consciousness of the environment. Drawing procures attention; it is a contemplative device.'

Writing and drawing are the representation of ideas in symbolic form. Compare the notion of a word and a line: both are internal ideas given an external, symbolic form. Drawing, like a written language, can be used as a tool of enquiry, comprehension and communication. The art teacher has a particular responsibility to provide the child with a different language system to order and understand experience.

If we consider drawing in relation to seeing as writing is to reading, we realize that the child simultaneously creates and uses his own language. It can be both a personal and a shared language, which the child should be encouraged to develop in order to investigate, understand, explain his experience to himself and others. Ralph Jeffery explains, 'I would like to see the growth in practice of drawing to the point where we could begin to think about the variety of functions, where we could use that language or mode of discourse in the same way we use verbal language in a number of different registers.'

Children's drawings should be viewed as evidence of a learning process. They are evidence of a search for meaning. Sources to which a child might refer are direct sensory experience, received images, memory and imagination (which of course are dependent on previous inputs of sensory information). The drawing may be seen as a reworking of these as the child attempts to find out, work out, understand or communicate.

Just as different kinds of written language serve different functions, we may use drawing for different reasons. For instance, company reports are not usually written in the form of poems, nor would one expect a letter from a friend to be written in the form of an election manifesto. We might also view drawing in the same way — in different contexts, different types of drawing serve different purposes. Drawing as analysis contributes to perceptual development in terms of receiving, organizing and interpreting sensory stimuli and discovering relationships between them. Drawing is a particular language which the child should learn in order to explain his experience to himself and others. It is a medium for developing perception, a way of communicating a feeling response. Drawing as communication involves the sharing of ideas, a realization of feeling and thinking processes, and an attempt to share them.

Communication may also imply that the pupil is able to relate more closely to the initial experience, or that the communication may be between the pupil and himself, in terms of understanding, coming to terms with the experience, and the ideas or feelings it generates. Or drawing may be the basis of interaction between the pupil and teacher, or between the pupil and others — the pupil has something to say with it. However, for successful communication, the message should be transmitted in a code and on a wavelength to someone capable of receiving it. Drawings need to be read and interpreted just like written language.

Annotated sketches are an effective and economic way of recording information and explaining a critical response to townscape. In townscape appraisal, both comprehension and use of a visual language is necessary, in order to understand townscape and to describe it. Art works can explain a subjective, affective response through the use of visual imagery, but do not necessarily communicate a critical appraisal. Criticism involves not only the making and expressing of value judgements, perhaps implicit in visual imagery, but an explanation or justification for those choices, which necessitate the use of written or verbal comments. The observer's meaning should be made explicit, so there can be no doubt what judgements were intended. Art teachers are familiar with the cartoon as a device which successfully combines visual and written elements. These also may be effectively used in the context of critical appraisal.

Photography

The use of the camera encourages purposeful looking. It can focus attention and direct observation. Photography is an excellent medium for scanning, for coping with a lot of information quickly, or for extracting detail and then relating it to its original context. In the Project photographs have not been seen as objective statements. They can express a personal, emotional response. Annotated photographs can explain a critical response. Photographs are of course also a useful way of storing

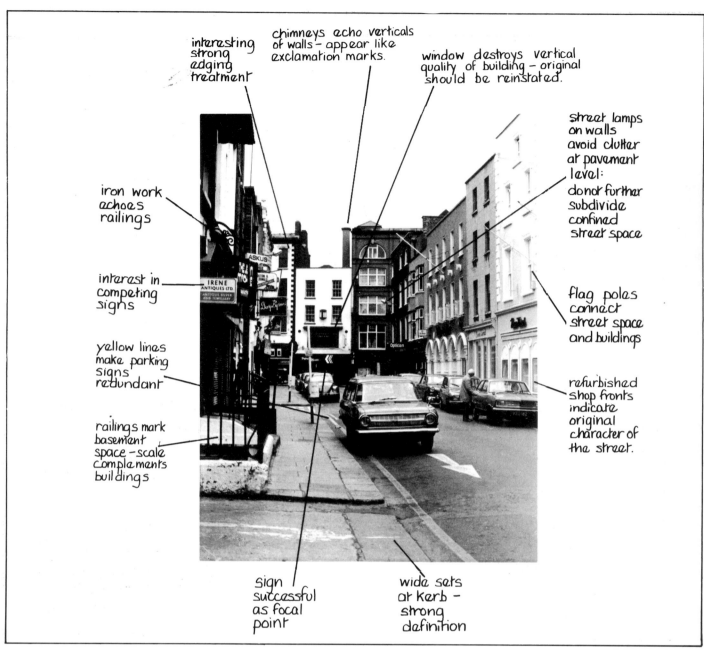

interesting strong edging treatment

chimneys echo verticals of walls – appear like exclamation marks.

window destroys vertical quality of building – original should be reinstated.

street lamps on walls avoid clutter at pavement level: do not further subdivide confined street space

iron work echoes railings

interest in competing signs

yellow lines make parking signs redundant

railings mark basement space – scale complements buildings

flag poles connect street space and buildings

refurbished shop fronts indicate original character of the street.

sign successful as focal point

wide sets at kerb – strong definition

recorded information. A collection may be built up over a period of time as a classroom resource for future reference by other pupils. Such a collection can also provide valuable documentation of a continually changing environment. Annotations may be used to make judgements explicit, to offer further explanation, to communicate evidence of discriminatory and critical skills. Photo collage can be used to suggest ideas for environmental improvements.

Slide programmes

Much photography in schools tends to be concerned with technical processes of developing and printing. Slides may be used by students who have little technical knowledge or as an introduction to photography. Because processing skills are not necessary, students can concentrate on the experience of townscape itself, and their response to it, rather than production skills. Their concern is more with the ideas they want to communicate.

Slides may be used to record information, which may be used later for reference, or as part of a programme which provides evidence for opinions and value judgements. With successive studies, schools will begin to build up a useful collection, which will become a valuable resource for both students and teachers, and can provide an introduction to a study of townscape, reference for work in progress, material for discussion or for further programmes. Students should keep records of their particular slides, and a central catalogue should document each slide. An index could indicate particular programmes or themes. Thus the initial outlay on film is recouped through the continued use of slides by successive groups of children.

We have often noticed a subsequent improvement in standards of work where pupils realize their work is of value and can be used by others. Their programmes may be used by other groups as a basis for enquiry or discussion. It is advisable to prepare tape commentaries for the programmes, as this obliges students to think more carefully about the ideas they wish to communicate. It is too easy to string together a number of images and call that a personal statement. The commentary permits the communication of a critical response.

making a slide programme

EXPLORATION

Explore the area to find out possibilities for study.

Collect as many ideas as possible.

Make notes through annotated sketches.

PREPARATION

Decide on a possible theme and time schedule.

Prepare a shooting plan or storyboard.

Further written notes may help with the commentary later on.

	STORYBOARD
	general streetscape
	individual houses
	Mrs Jones washing windows
	interviewing Mrs Jones
	back garden – washing line
	garden shed rubbish

INVESTIGATION

Using storyboard as a guide take slides of locations.
Make written notes, giving as much information as possible.

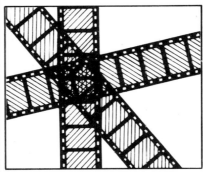

Take more slides than you will need, so you will have a few shots to select from. All the slides can be kept in a general collection anyway and used later for other purposes.

INTERPRETATION

Label your slides – do they have a collection catalogue number?
Sort them out.
Do they suggest any further ideas for the programme or alternative approaches?
Do you need any other slides?
What are you trying to say?
Does the programme need captions or a commentary?

You may want to use clips from interview in the commentary.
Prepare the necessary questions.
Test your equipment.
Try and find good conditions for recording.

You will need to edit any tape recording for your programme.
How long do you stay with one slide?

COMMUNICATION

What are the main ideas you are trying to put across?
Is the programme comprehensible?
Who is your intended audience?
Is the programme entertaining/educational/informative?
How do you know when to change slides?
Does it need any intro-duction or explanation?
Is it too long/short/quick/slow?
Test it out on some friends.

Part Three:
Trial runs

Work with teachers and students

The 4 chapters which follow describe in some detail the experience of some of the schools associated with the Project, firstly as part of the A-level Art course, secondly as the focus of fieldwork, thirdly as a General Studies course, and finally as work in the Art Department for the 11–16 age range in secondary education.

To avoid unnecessary repetition we present accounts of the ideas, organization and study methods of a characteristic range of schools and colleges rather than that of every one of our trial institutions. These had been selected on the basis of their variety, as well of course on that of their willingness to experiment. There were schools operating a 'core curriculum', single sex and mixed schools, and a Welsh-speaking school. There were different departmental structures — art department, design department, faculty of creative studies, and so on. And there were very varied local environments: new town, dying village, inner city, suburb and housing estate.

The important variables in developing environmental work appeared to us to be the members of staff who might contribute to the study: the support offered to the teacher by the head; the connections made with agencies outside the school — with architects and planners and subject advisers; and in particular, the school timetable. (Did it provide for large enough blocks of time for streetwork to be possible? Was it flexible enough in the sixth form for students to work together?)

In the schools the work was incorporated into existing Art or General Studies courses. In preparing schemes of work the kind of question teachers found themselves asking were:

What courses are appropriate?
How might they be incorporated into the existing curriculum?
What should the context of these courses be?
What balance should there be between streetwork and classwork?
What should the balance be between input from the teacher and personal research by the pupil?
How much time should be given to this type of study?
How does it relate to examinations?
How can it fit into a General Studies course?
Which study area should be selected?
Is one location more appropriate than others?
What resources will be needed?
What special expertise is necessary?
What learning activites are appropriate for different ages?

12 A-level Art

In the trial schools the art courses for the 16–19 age range were geared towards A-level Art examinations. Most teachers interpreted the syllabuses as being concerned primarily with the control of expressive media, production skills and the development of a visual language as a means of expression. Some courses were also concerned with aspects of art history and architectural history, but few seemed to promote critical studies or to give particular attention to environmental study. All the trial schools involved their A-level Art groups in Project work to some extent and many of the teachers would agree that the experience served to enrich and enhance the students' work in other areas of art studies. Some A-level Art courses emphasized the need to explore and to experiment, while others put much more emphasis on producing finished pieces of work to build up a portfolio. Most teachers accepted that the experience of art making was the basis of their work, though they admitted that more time and attention should be paid to the development of critical skills. Overall we found the A-level Art and Design courses heavily biased towards the manipulation of media and the acquisition of craft skills.

Our experience of A-level Art courses in the trial schools has convinced us that the syllabuses can quite happily support environmental work and that the work is complementary to other areas of study within A-level Art courses.

Peter Symonds College

Peter Symonds College is a sixth form college at Winchester. Art education there is promoted within the Creative Arts Faculty which includes fine art and technical studies. 4 art teachers provide courses whose main

	Art and the built environment	1st year A level art	2nd year A level art
Experience	experience of the environment discriminatory and critical skills derived from environmentally based aesthetic experience	experience of a wide range of media discriminatory skills derived from media based aesthetic experience	experience of the artist's approach particular media skills developed
Research	recording information through sketchbooks, diaries, journals, collections also – assessment sheets, tape recordings, photography		
	emphasis on subjective, affective responses to environment	emphasis on expressive possibilities of media	emphasis on expressive skills
Study techniques	assessment exercises critical skills based on analysis – assessment appraisal, synthesis-evaluation emphasis on the ability to make and explain value judgements	(expressive) visual language exercises, communicatory skills based on control and exploitation of media emphasis on exploration and experiment with expressive media and communication skills	long term projects chosen and developed by individual students emphasis on the development of personal insight
Received knowledge	comparison of personal perceptions with those of others emphasis on personal experience as a basis for comparison	history of art relationship of art and society emphasis on the work of recognised artists	A-level History of Art: history of painting 1780–1860, history of architecture 1780–1860: general topics planning and architecture

components are painting, 3-dimensional work, ceramics and photography. Students have come from a variety of previous schools in a large catchment area and represent a wide range of ability and experience in art. The main considerations for acceptance on the A-level Art course are interest in the subject and a personal commitment to the work. Qualities like self-motivation, initiative and persistence are fundamental to the ethos of the college and this ethos is reflected in the policies adopted by the art department.

The department's stated policy is that in the first year of the course members of staff are

'more concerned with visual education than the production of works of art. They see one of their main problems as breaking down preconceptions of what art is about, and encouraging an inquisitive attitude towards visual problems and ideas through both calculated processes and intuitive reactions. The course is dynamic in that it changes from year to year, but it relies on the primary use of the visual world as a starting point, source and basic vocabulary from which to select specific problems or on which to impose personal ideas or feelings. The core is reflected in the studies involving drawing and abstraction, and these, together with an introduction to different processes and techniques, and an investigation of visual language, are the essence of the first year scheme.'

In the second year, students are encouraged to develop more personal approaches to study and to take greater responsibility for the development of their own work. They are expected to undertake a major study lasting 5 months, from January to June, as staff believe that an important part of the sixth form experience should be the challenge to define, develop and sustain a major project over a long period.

The art course at the College may be described as an attempt to teach aspects of the language of art through practical studies, together with some historical theoretical background. There is a development and change of emphasis during the 2 year course: the visual language exercises set by teachers during the first year give way to these longer term individual projects chosen by the students themselves.

The earlier emphasis on experiment with different media gives way to concentration on a more limited range to develop personal preferences and strengths. In the first year, critical studies are incorporated informally through discussions about the work in progress in relation to a wider knowledge of art: in the second year, more attention is given to the demands of the A-level History of Art syllabus, and entails more concentration on the building up of a body of knowledge.

ABE work in relation to A-level Art

The diagram (left) explains the areas of concern common to both ABE work and A-level Art at Peter Symonds College. It may be seen that there are strong connections which can be made between the 2 areas, though the emphasis and the bias of the work may be quite different.

There is however no need to consider ABE work as separate and distinct from A-level Art, for the emphasis and bias of one can only enrich and promote the strengths of the other.

As may be seen, the ABE work gave an added dimension to the work already undertaken for the A-level Art examination. It became apparent that, although certain ideas were important to both, it was perhaps the bias of the concern that differed:

Experience — *in the case of A-level Art, experience of media or the artist's working methods were felt to be very important; whereas in ABE work, study is based firmly on experience of the environment.*

Research — *in the case of A-level Art, much time was spent in experiment with the expressive possibilities of various media. Ideas were developed from a knowledge and control of media. In ABE work, ideas were developed from an enlarged response to the environment.*

Study techniques — *both the A-level Art and ABE work were geared to the study of an adequate working vocabulary to cope with the demands of the respective studies, and the ability to develop personal insight. The Art syllabus promoted exercises concerned with visual communication; ABE work promoted those concerned with assessment and judgement of townscape.*

Knowledge — *although ABE work is generally promoted as a practical study based on direct experience of the environment, there is a need for students to compare their perceptions with those of others, and to consider possible explanations, judgements, opinions outside their own experience. Art and architectural history are not usually presented as a collection of opinions, and students are generally unaware how selective the 'body of knowledge' with which they are presented is.*

The nature of the work

The art teachers felt that the ABE Project ideas should be incorporated in the framework of A-level Art rather than be set apart as a separate and special area of study. It was thus related to ideas of personal maturity and visual awareness that permeated the A-level Art study. The policy of the art department for the first year sixth was to encourage pupils to explore unfamiliar media or aspects of visual language. The environment was used as a focus for this study, but, at first, students' concepts of art excluded the type of work in critical appraisal the Project sought to promote.

The first ABE studies included short, specific projects which fitted the broad structure of the art course, but which were slanted in an attempt to accommodate the demands of the Project. These included studies on movement, figure as sculpture, structures. Individual studies selected and developed by students over a longer period of time included barriers, contrast, change, minimal buildings, windows. This repeated the approach of selecting specific themes and manipulating them for personal and artistic ends rather than the selection being based on particular townscape areas and the study displaying discriminatory and critical skills in relation to the environment rather than in relation to the use of expressive media.

Encountering the unfamiliar

The students found it difficult to know how to tackle an art-based environmental study. The emphasis was very much on using the environment as stimulus, as reference, as a source of ideas and material for art work; they tended to select details or restricted visual problems, remove them from their context and seek to develop a personal statement in the art studio, transforming the environmental starting point into something else divorced from its original context.

They were initially very heavily influenced by their previous experience of environmental studies on other subjects, and had no suitable model from their art studies which they could apply to a critical study of the environment. They felt the need for a scientific approach or were dominated by historical, sociological or geographical modes, and assumed that an urban study *must* involve surveys, statistics, questionnaires and interviews. There was also some confusion about the need to be subjective: students felt that only objectivity was permissible.

It was difficult for students to sustain momentum and concentration in this relatively unfamiliar area of study. Winter weather conditions initially hampered opportunities for streetwork and for collecting information. College examinations and other projects also affected the pace of development of the study. Students found it difficult to focus on particular aspects, to define and isolate a particular problem, continually discovering alternative possibilites for study.

Some teachers felt that it was an imposition on an already full course; that it should be aimed at a younger age group, and did not necessarily relate to 'the complexity and relatively advanced thinking of students at 16 + level.' Some, too, felt that the work involved 'too much thought and explanation rather than experience of art.'

Influencing A-level work

After a full 2 year involvement in the ABE research, Peter Symonds College has gone some way to establishing a case for greater consideration of the need for critical studies within the A-level Art course.

The art teachers reported that although students (new to the college and with a miscellany of previous experiences) found it difficult at first to relate the demands of the Project to their expectations of the art course, it did provide an excellent opportunity to explore their ideas and preconceptions about art, and to discuss what they hoped to gain from the course as a whole. It also demonstrated that although teachers were concerned to modify students' preconceptions about art, they themselves cherished certain expectations and preconceptions that strongly determined the nature of the art course, and some of them were not so keen to relinquish them.

Students began by finding it difficult to develop environmental work in their early studies but a number of them returned to it in their second year, when there were more opportunities for developing their own projects. In the A-level examination about a fifth of the students in the art course produced work based on the ideas developed in the Project. The environmental work undertaken by the students has, in fact, complemented their normal art studies and has developed and enlarged their understanding, rather than intruding on valuable working time as was originally feared.

After initial doubts and problems, students developed not only a greater awareness and a critical response to the environment, but perhaps a better understanding of the role of art in developing perception. The head of the department feels that it has become increasingly apparent that some form of analytical and critical study should be an important part of the A-level syllabus: 'There needs to be scope for the development of an area which could link the history of art with the "middle ground" of both subjective and objective analysis and criticism through written and visual statements.'

Their previous experience had led the students to understand art only as a vehicle for expression, and they could not perceive its possibilities as an investigatory tool or a means of analysis. Only as the Project developed did students begin to appreciate that they could react intuitively and directly to the built environment without necessarily having to resort to the kind of systematic research and calculated approach promoted by scientific modes of study. They needed to develop confidence and skill in using art as an experiential, analytical and expressive medium to explore their responses to the built environment.

A-level work

The illustrations (right) show the kinds of work, produced as a part of the Project, which fit easily into the characteristic content of an A-level portfolio. Here the environment is used as reference and a basis for analysis. In the majority of cases the emphasis is on visual qualities but the illustration at bottom right shows the sound pattern of a particular place presented in visual terms, while the painting of the cathedral interior explores the spatial relationships between people and a building.

A-level work demands that teachers and students look beyond the finished products to understand the meaning of the processes involved. The sequence on the right demonstrates one way in which this can happen and shows the importance of the 'difficulties' thrown up by an attempt to make art from an analysis of the environment. At each stage the problems encountered have suggested the next step in development. The illustrations on the right show:

1 *Initial rough sketch of part of a building site seen through a viewfinder*
2 *More detailed observation of objects*
3 *Interest in spatial relationships*
4 *Further exploration of spatial relationships*
5 *Tentative attempt to illustrate 3-dimensional properties*
6 *Maquette exploring 3-dimensional relationships more adequately*
7 *Full-scale sculpture*

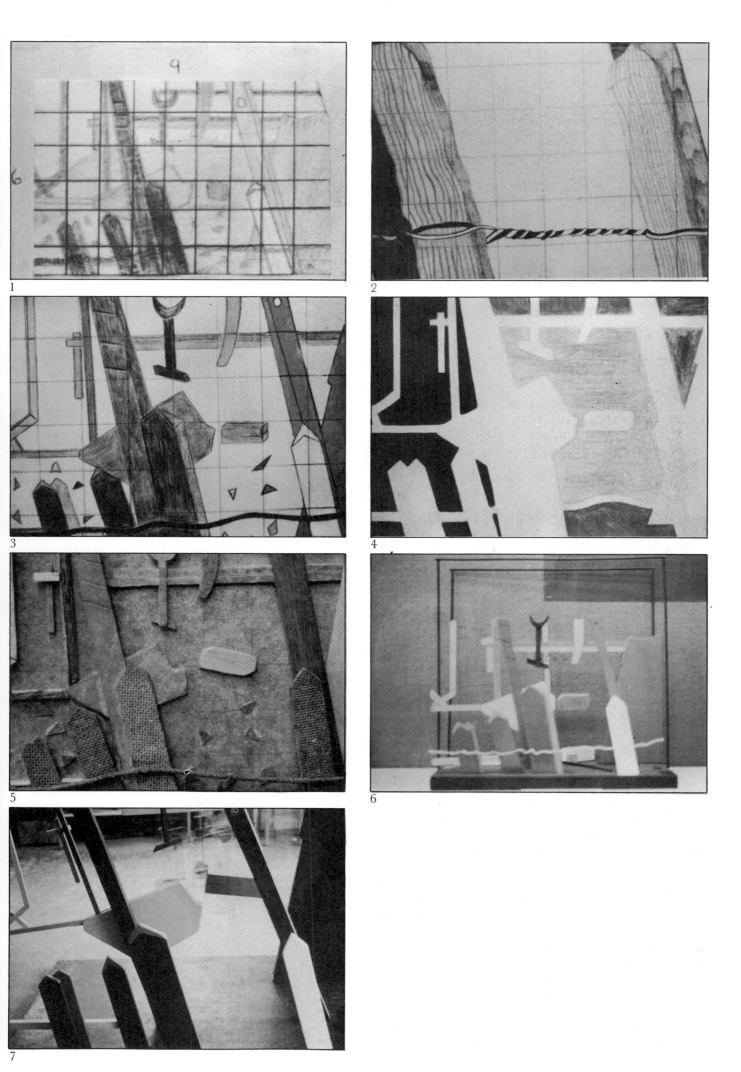

1
2
3
4
5
6
7

97

Rotherham College of Arts and Community Studies

The course at Rotherham College of Arts and Community Studies known as General Education Through Art and Design (GEAD) aims to integrate basic art and design elements with academic vocational studies: it builds a general education around art. For this reason we chose to study this course at this further education college to compare it with other A-level provision in schools.

GEAD was established in the Yorkshire and Humberside region in 1972, and is designed as a 2 year course for students leaving school at 16 + . Over the 2 years, 70% of the time is spent on art and design and the remainder of the time is given to general education. In practice, this means that the students spend Tuesday, Wednesday and Thursday in studio work, while Monday and Friday are devoted to English, history and social studies. At the end of the course successful students are awarded a certificate and normally take a number of O- and A-level examinations, including an Art and Craft A-level.

Entry to the course is by interview and consideration of the student's folio of work. The course is designed to meet the needs of a minority of 16–18 year olds which are not adequately met in secondary schools. By integrating basic art and design elements with academic and vocational studies it is thought possible to provide the student with an incentive to continue formal education and possibly the

In these examples the emphasis is on creating powerful and dramatic images from the environment. They also show how students have been prepared to look afresh at familiar surroundings and revalue those things we all tend to take for granted.

opportunity to apply for more advanced courses of study and gain better employment prospects. The course is based upon the strengths of these students in art and design and aims to link these with other subjects in a wider educational context.

The stated aim of the course is

'to provide a framework for study within which a student can discover and develop his full potential through working in areas normally associated with the creative arts. Students are encouraged to develop a capacity for independent inquiry and an ability to express conclusions based on personal research. The staff hope to develop in the student an ability to think and communicate more easily through the use of spoken and written English as well as visual media of drawing and photography.'

The first year of the course is based on projects suggested by the teacher, which may link studies on other areas, techniques and production skills in relation to media and academic study for other GCE subjects. In the second year students continue with these other studies and develop a major art/design project intended to deepen their study in a particular area.

The artist's view

During the period of association between the course and our Project the study environments chosen by students have included the route to the college (a sensory walk), the home and its environs, the neighbourhood (for example a study of the village of Treeton, tracing its development from an agricultural hamlet to an industrial suburb as seen through the eyes of the miners who had lived there from childhood), a study of cemeteries ('The Victorian Way of Death'), fairgrounds and housing estates. Study methods included some suggested by the Project, like the exploration of serial vision (see page 000).

The GEAD work at Rotherham certainly displays a high level of technical skill and personal commitment. Students have exploited the built environment as an infinite source of ideas for their work. They were also able to make use of a number of exploratory exercises developed for the Project by Keith Wheeler and Brian Goodey. Their work demonstrates a personal, emotional response to a range of environmental stimuli, and some of it, like the Treeton study and the work of the student who explored 'The Victorian Way of Death', shows a high level of sensitivity and understanding.

What we did not find was the development of specific critical capacities in relation to particular townscapes. In this, and in other similar courses, as in most schools, the strong bias towards the production of fine art objects, tends, in our view, to inhibit the development of critical studies in relation to the environment as these do not necessarily result in recognizable art products which can be hung on a gallery wall.

In this as in other similar courses the favoured study model was that of the artist solving problems through the manipulation of expressive media. Students' judgements were implicit in the art work and there was little attempt at further explanation or justification. In any case discrimination and judgement were usually applied in response to the image or art object or to the most appropriate use of media or to a technical problem of production rather than in relation to the environment itself.

An interesting point is the selection of study environments — what constituted environment to the students and what they chose to portray. They tended to choose either the prosaic and domestic (the interior of home, the garden path, back door and shed) or the exotic (sports stadium, tram museum, fairground and cemetery). Their minds were on image-making and the picturesque, in spite of the efforts of tutors to direct them towards streetscape, the journey to college, and so on. It is hard for students, whether in school or college, to make the leap from producing conventional set pieces to applying a seeing eye to the whole environment.

The series of drawings applies the close, closer, closest test to the domestic environment of the kitchen but could just as easily be used in the context of the street to investigate the experience of serial vision.

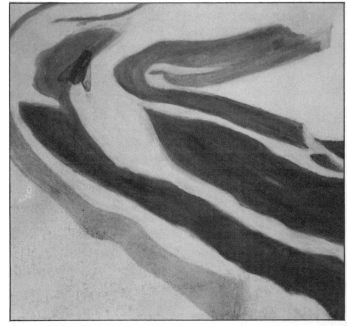

A sensory walk offered a useful introduction to exploring and observing. These 2 examples show clearly how varying experiences and responses contribute to different individual perceptions.

This collection of work formed part of studies by 2 students which illuminated the cultural background to an aspect of environment by focussing on the interaction between people, their customs and symbolic objects.

Part of a girl's study of her home, the industrialized suburb of Treeton. She traced its development from an agricultural hamlet as seen through the eyes of the miners who had lived there since boyhood. The study included paintings, photographs, interviews, the production of a book and perspex reliefs.

Banbury School

Banbury School, Oxfordshire, was the largest comprehensive school in our study. Although part of the design faculty, the art department preserves its own identity and autonomy, so the work demonstrated a fine art bias. The Project work at this school reflected the personal interest and enthusiasm of a single teacher — and, as is so often the case with innovatory work, continuity was broken when he left the school. Fortunately, personal research involving exploration, investigation, observation and recording information forms the basis for much of the A-level Art work done at the school in any case. The Project offered an incentive to exploit the environment more fully, and to provide an added dimension to the work through the demands of critical study.

Emotional responses

An art field trip to a village in Devon provided an excellent opportunity for experiment with a range of working methods suitable for an art based environmental study. The time and seclusion permitted students to work on problems without the usual distractions of a busy school life, and gave them the chance to work with a different range of ideas and media than those usually considered in the art studio.

The experience gained during the field work encouraged them to explore the more familiar environment of their own locality. The canal study involved a general exploration, where students were asked to work independently, to find various ways of recording different kinds of information. They were then asked to focus more closely on particular aspects which interested them, and to develop a piece of work based on their *feelings* about the place. We reproduce (see pages 104-105) the texts of the study brief issued to the students by the art teacher, Anthony Morgan. This is a way of working familiar to many art departments, though not all of them would have attempted the other parts of the study brief, which asked for a piece of work using materials found in the environment and for some modification to be made to the environment.

As far as critical appraisal was concerned, students at Banbury, as elsewhere, seemed to be more interested in what the environment had to offer as a basis for image-making than in attempting to comment on it directly, or to make judgements about other things than its picturesque potential and then to explain these judgements.

Students seemed more concerned to present an explanation of their activity than to present an explanation of the results of that activity. The teacher felt that the students' work resulted in a predominantly romantic interpretation of the canal area. There was evidence of their projecting their own fantasies on to the environment as well as receiving ideas from it: for example, the configuration of water surface patterns and reflections. They were also attracted to the broken-down and decrepit areas, which perhaps offered more scope for fantasy. This art teacher firmly believes that the development of

capacities for imagination and fantasy are fundamental to deepening people's perception of the environment.

Students' comments confirm their preoccupation with imaginative reconstruction:

'Discovering two bottles on the canal bank, I felt although they actually polluted the canal, they did not appear out of context with the environment. Nature is only partially tamed by human intervention, because eventually the man-made objects, the canal and everything connected with it, become overwhelmed by nature. Intending to portray this relationship, the final artwork is a juxtaposition of the two conflicting elements. The background attempts to evoke the sun, sky and cornfields, in contrast to the man-made canal, drains and bottles.'
DONNA BURTON

'After exploring the canal area I found myself drawn to the main bridge. I liked the reflection under the bridge on the water and the apparent circle it made in conjunction with the inner arch of the bridge. I made several sketches of this, using bold, flat colours because the canal area seemed dead and totally devoid of life. My work progressed from the reflections to a footpath. I was interested in its smooth contours and unusual shapes — I included this element in my final painting. I also included rock surfaces and some wire which I found visually interesting. After experimenting with various media, I decided to use brown water colour and black ink. I had originally thought of the canal as an uninspiring place, but after several visits it became a problem to confine my visual interest to one area only.'
JOHN MALONEY

'On my first visit to the canal I noticed the water's edge, the difference between one area and another: one well looked after and the other in a poor state of repair and littered with debris. But how to show this? I originally thought of the edge of the water — in some places, clear, sharp reflections, in others a raft of litter upon murky water. I eventually made up a piece of work which presented the conflicting ramshackle buildings, and in the centre the origin of both: the canal.'
COLIN BRADLEY

'On our first visit to the canal I became interested in the operation of the lock gates. I find the gates characteristic of the canal. I chose the subject of dirty, oily ratchet mechanisms which control the flow of water on which the canal depends.'
MARTIN HILL

'Having studied the canal area I became aware of and interested in the water as a visual phenomenon. What I have done in my artwork is to take, out of context, the patterns of water, by freezing a moment in its continuous happening. Then using this frozen image to make a painting which is a representation of the surface of the water.'
BRYAN KIRKPATRICK

'My idea was not to represent reality but to combine what I found in the canal in order to project an image of what can be seen at the site. I started with the brickwork as that seemed to be the basis of the canal and the surrounding area. I then concentrated on the vegetation. The canal itself ended up being the last element to be included as it seemed to be just passing through.'   SUE CLEAVER

'My first impression of the canal was of a place of decay, created and exploited by industry. The canal itself was silent and cold, very uninviting, yet it had a power. On the canal bank there were several work yards, each with its own array of junk. It was one of these that caught my eye at first. It seemed to be indicative of all the canal meant to me. I began my work with simple pen and ink studies of the yard and the objects in it. At this early stage I had in mind a conventional finished piece of artwork. However, as I progressed I came to the conclusion that a simple representational picture of the canal bank would fail to capture the feelings I had. So I took some simple line drawings of the yard and began to experiment by scribbling, tearing and even burning them in an attempt to express my feelings. Finally I began to work along lines I had never explored before. These led to my finished piece. It is quite different from my previous work. I feel however that it is a success in that it does reflect the mood of the canal. The burnt sketch, torn newspaper and grey spray paint do express my feelings about the canal environment. Although some of the elements in the work are not directly concerned with the canal, they still harmonize with the mood.' ROBERT STRACHAN

The idea of creating a piece of work from materials found in the environment which is then left there, encourages students to get to grips with the environment and sense it in more ways than the simply visual. The objects produced remain as a record of their experience and may possibly communicate something about that environment (if merely mystification) to the passer-by. The art teacher found that this approach releases students from preconceptions and constraints they might normally feel in an art study. Anthony Morgan claims:

'Insensitivity to our environment is largely the contempt bred by familiarity. To have our frame of reference suddenly jolted by the presence of something in a place which is not normally there, such as environmental artwork, can bring into focus again how we regard the place in which it exists.'

Students explain their response to this particular study task:

'Under the arch of a bridge, we found some old bricks and decided that it would be apt if we could construct a model of the front of a narrow boat just under the arch. We could see the light reflecting on the water from the other side of the bridge and decided that the spectator should look through the boat from the front at the highly contrasting reflections behind. We chose the narrow boat as the symbol of the canal's existence to parallel the dereliction we found in the area. We gave the boat the name 'Bathania' as we thought this typical of the names given to such boats.'   MARTIN HILL

'Along the canal bank there was a huge amount of waste and man-made clutter. There was a strong feeling of dirt and ugliness on the bank in contrast to the surreal beauty of the reflections on the water surface. The pieces I used were positioned to reflect the semi-organized clutter which the environment was.'
BRYAN KIRKPATRICK

'The weather on the morning we went to the canal was wet and dreary. As a result I decided I wanted to show an ugly aspect of the canal: litter. I found an area down in a river flood outlet. The place was dark, damp, sheltered and full of rubbish. I attempted to take this aspect to an extreme by creating a new breed of 'man' which grows out of rubbish, devouring it for nourishment.'   COLIN BRADLEY

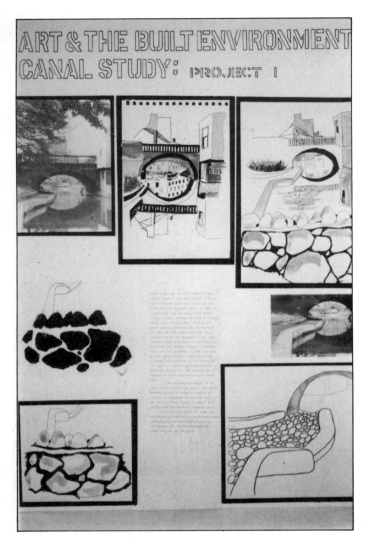

The canal study

The brief for the study shown here has been taken from the teacher's brief:

The intention of the projects is to use the canal area as a factor in the production of artwork, thus encouraging understanding of this environment and sensitivity to its qualities.

It is intended that you should DISCOVER WHAT YOU FEEL about the place you are making a study of. You will be using the medium of visual art to discover and communicate these feelings.

Some starting points:

1 Details of construction, e.g. gates, walls, machinery, buildings, decoration, boats, etc.
2 Surfaces of things, e.g. natural objects, man-made objects, water, etc.
3 Wild life and vegetation, e.g. seeds, flowers, trees, butterflies, flies, insects, fungi, etc.
4 Extraneous materials, e.g. scrap, rubbish, etc.

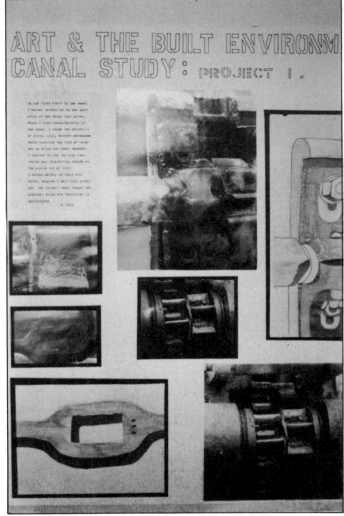

Project A

1   *Initial investigation (worksheet):*
a visit location.
b make records of response to the area.
(drawings, notes, maps, diagrams, etc.).
c take photographs.
d bring back to school an object that has
emotive significance, relationship to the
location or any other connection.

2   *Research into artform (studio):*
Proceeding from the investigatory/record
materials or retrieved objects, produce an
object (can take any form — 2-D, 3-D,
mixed media etc.) that reflects, or makes a
comment or statement on, the location.
Alternatively, produce an artwork that is
derived (however obscurely) from the record
materials and retrieved items or is the result
of stimulus provided by the location.

Project B

Location artwork:
This project consists of producing an artwork that
forms an actual part of the environment of the
location. The object of the work:
a highlight a quality or qualities of the location.
b make a statement on the nature of the location.
c is a result of a stimulus provided by the location.

Ideally these pieces of work are seen as being left *in
situ*. Where this is not practicable, photographs and
other records could be made.

Study subjects included materials (use, weathering), natural form (in relation to built form), the village shop (ideas for improvement), barriers (a study of 'defensible space'), modern buildings, streetscape, and minimal buildings (huts, sheds, barns). The study was an investigation of a variety of structures and spaces and how people used them. This showed how the village had changed from being a focus for a farming community to a largely residential area.

13 Field studies

School timetables do not always provide the most convenient time allocations for environmental work. Hour-long sessions are hardly adequate as streetwork demands 2–hour or half-day sessions. Schools which operate block timetable arrangements have found it easier to accommodate streetwork, as have those which possess a minibus. Travel to and from study sites can take up valuable lesson time. Over-exploitation of the local area can also be a problem, so alternative study sites should be considered, to offer different environmental experiences and an opportunity for comparison.

An obvious way of enlarging environmental experience is to make comparative studies of the home environment and a completely different one. The provision of rural centres for urban schools is a valuable resource for art teachers, but has been under-exploited by them. Even when schools do not have regular access to these, local authorities and other agencies can provide suitable accommodation. The growth of the movement for urban studies centres can provide the opposite kind of contrast.

Field studies have traditionally been the province of the biologist and the geographer who are well aware of their educational advantages. Art teachers might consider their potential for a continuous period of work providing for depth of study and the opportunity to develop a study over a period of time without interruption. This encourages a greater understanding of art as a medium for both expression and perception. The change of location offers a range of experience and stimuli not available in the art studio. In a recent ILEA exhibition of work from various rural centres, the bulk of the work was concerned with identification and quantification, based on scientific modes of study. Art was used merely as illustration, as a means of escape to the romantic idyll of the countryside, or as a release from the pressures of 'real' work. But just as science imposes its own discipline of study methods and ways of understanding, art can also be a means of encouraging observation, analysis, comparison and judgement.

A number of schools involved in the work of the Project reported on their field visits of 1, 2 or 7 days' duration. Not only did these provide opportunities to study unfamiliar environments, they also encouraged fresh perceptions of familiar areas.

A 1–day field visit to a beach to study natural form gave pupils from Ysgol Gyfun, Ystalyfera, an opportunity to compare this with a study of the built environment. Study methods they developed on the beach were then applied to the local village, and work developed from their observations. This linked with the art department's policy of varying study environments and building up a range of environmental experiences and study methods.

The beach trip was useful for it encouraged the natural urge to explore, to discover, to touch, collect, compare, manipulate and to share experience. As was the case with many field visits the excitement and strangeness of a new place raised levels of anticipation and awareness and encouraged a fresh look at a familiar environment. Pupils made a slide programme, using the fantastic shapes of the rocks and imagining how they had evolved. Images of actual rock formations were interspersed with pupils' work, and were accompanied by music and a narration of pupils' comments and poetry. This first attempt by younger children provided ideas for the older students' initial programme on the village, where the visual images were of the present dying village and the commentary built up of recordings of old people's recollections of what the village used to be like.

Both groups discovered ways of looking, observing, making notes, through visual and tactile approaches — clambering, handling, collecting, sketching, rubbing and photographing — and were keen to apply these techniques to a totally different kind of place. The value of the visit to a completely different kind of environment is in sharpening perceptions of a familiar one which can be observed with a fresh eye.

Kingsthorpe School

Kingsthorpe Upper School's study of a Northampton village lasted only a week-end, but the long working sessions and the opportunity for concentrated study offered opportunity for continuity and depth of study that would not have been possible under normal school working conditions, where distractions or other commitments interfere. A rural studies centre which had once been the village school served as the study base, and the group of 12 students looked after themselves. Both fifth- and sixth-formers were involved and the work gave them a greater insight into the possibilities of art as a serious study. It involved streetwork, studio sessions and discussions, and encouraged students to develop to a greater extent than is possible under normal timetable conditions. They were asked to observe the village not as a source for visual imagery or for the making of works of art, but as a study of various townscape effects, considering how they had arisen or how they had been achieved. It was intended that ideas discovered during the fieldwork should be further developed back at school.

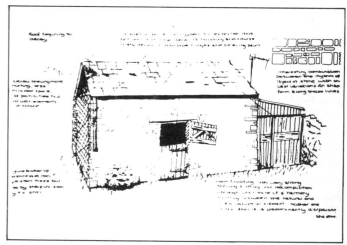

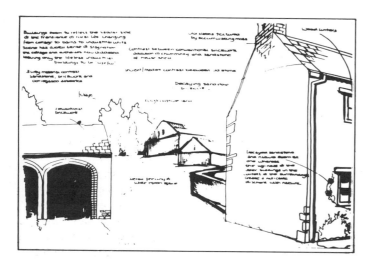

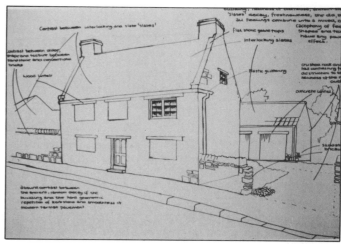

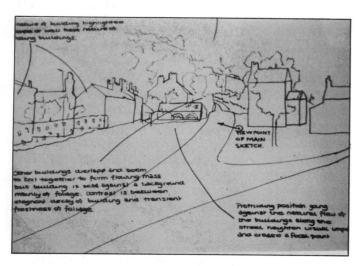

This set of drawings shows how one student started with an artist's response to the village, seeing buildings isolated as material for picture-making. The student then began to consider the way in which the buildings were constructed, how they were placed in relation to other buildings and spaces, and how they enhanced or detracted from the villagescape.

However, the work tended to remain at the level of picturesque composition until students began to think critically about these subjects in the context of the village-scape, how they related to other elements: the other buildings and the spaces in between, and whether they contributed to or detracted from the visual and spatial qualities of the place. The purpose of the drawing activity then changed from that of producing attractive images to that of documenting relationships to explain the aesthetic qualities apparent. The character of the drawing also changed, in that mark-making was reduced to essential information necessary to explain particular points of criticism. Further comment was expressed through written annotations.

Some of the subjects lent themselves more readily than others to critical study. One was that of the village store, a small new building set back from the main street and destroying its visual and textural rhythm through its position and its building materials. Another was the theme of other forms of modern development in an old setting: new bungalows, houses and garages and their relation to the older buildings in style and scale. Both these offered scope for alternative views and ideas for improvements. There was not time to complete such studies over the week-end, but students were able to develop them in their own time or in later school sessions. Also, study methods adopted on the field trip were applied to other environments. For instance, one student made a critical appraisal of his own village — annotated drawings were used to describe and comment on individual buildings and photographs to explain the context. The field work contributed to further development in art and design studies later and formed part of his A-level work submitted for the examination. Thus ways of researching developed on the field study which could be adapted for other studies.

Meal times offered an opportunity for students and teachers to discuss the work in progress. At first, students wished to prepare other work for display, to 'tidy up' sketches, but quickly got used to the idea that initial sketches were valuable evidence and should not be altered in the studio to make them more easily understood, but should be used as reference, as rough notes for further statements. Teachers, too, joined in the streetwork, and provided valuable models for the students to see how studies of this kind might be tackled. They submitted their drawings for comment, explained how they had approached the work, and the various techniques and devices they used to organize and communicate information. This sharing of experience and ideas, and the need to explain working activities and value judgements, was another valuable aspect of the course.

It was also useful to have teachers arguing publicly about particular points of interpretation. Because there was no generally acceptable 'correct' response, students were obliged to make up their own minds and decide on their own particular opinion and the reasons for it. The strongest argument concerned the character of the village — whether it could be regarded as a working rural community or merely as an urban dormitory. This led to discussion on living patterns and the changing environment, with consideration of future possibilities.

Priory School

Priory School in Portsmouth used a church hall in a Somerset village as their base for a week's field trip. Staff were accommodated at the vicarage and students used the hall as a dormitory at night and a workroom during the day. A kitchen and washroom were available and there was ample exhibition space where work was displayed and discussed in 'crit. sessions' every day.

The working day was divided into 4 sessions — 1 in the morning, 2 in the afternoon and 1 in the evening. The choice of July was good — excellent weather, no examination pressures, and away from the end-of-term school atmosphere. The students worked long and hard. These students in the first year of the sixth form had already been involved in an art-based study of Portsmouth. This had been particularly concerned with developing awareness and observation, but had not emphasized critical appraisal. The village study was not concerned with the environment as a basis for visual imagery, but sought to promote discriminatory and critical capacities.

16 students travelled by minibus after school on Friday and set up equipment and materials in the hall. 3 members of the art department, together with their families, accompanied the group on the first week-end and after that 2 teachers remained with the group. It was a very busy, cooperative atmosphere, and the extra help provided by teachers' wives was much appreciated in setting up domestic arrangements. Students had been involved in the planning of the week and shared transport and food costs, while the school paid for hire of the hall.

The first study session that evening was an introduction to the work through a slide programme. Although students were tired after a week at school, it was thought best to plunge straight into the study and present them with a range of ideas and problems at the very beginning when there was a high level of interest and excitement, so that they could start on their streetwork on the following morning. This proved a good decision as it imposed certain expectations and a pace of working which affected the whole study. Those students who had expected a quiet week in the country involving a little sketching and some landscape painting were suddenly confronted with a range of ideas, considerations, questions and examples which they had not anticipated and which encouraged a fresh outlook and a heightened anticipation. So they were eager to start work next day.

The work on the first day was a series of observation studies concerned with selecting and recording information on spatial qualities quickly and economically. At first students were naturally attracted to the picturesque detail and were more interested in drawing pleasing objects like church gates and wisteria around doorways than in understanding spatial relationships. The first 'crit. session' offered a good opportunity for teachers to find out what the students' initial approach had been, and what the problems were. Some of the girls found the concept of space a hard one to grasp at first. However, it was continually stressed that the scope of the study was much greater than recording information: choices and preferences had to be explained, and everything should be

Serial vision in a country lane.

seen in the context of the streetscape or landscape in which it stood, so that objects should be related to each other and to the space which they created.

The teacher in charge of the course, Roger Standen, devised a series of games to overcome the difficulties felt by some students. This imaginative approach had several advantages. Skittles, snakes and ladders, Monopoly and so on are all built round movement, either in space or on a board, and this brought home the dynamic element of environmental exploration. Secondly, the gaming approach overcame diffidence or anxiety, and thirdly of course it was fun, while students of this age were sufficiently distanced from childhood games to see the purpose behind the exercises.

Contact had been made with the vicar, through one of the art teachers, to arrange for acccomodation, but neither students nor residents knew quite what to expect from each other. The students' interest in the village and their obvious commitment to the work intrigued the children from the local primary school, who wanted to know more about it, so they were invited to join in one afternoon. The whole village was invited to the display of work in the village hall, and among the people attending were residents from both the old cottages and the new developments, who joined in the discussion about their environment. The school has been invited to return next year and the headmaster of the primary school has asked to arrange a course for his pupils.

This kind of outcome cannot be arranged or planned: it is simply the spin-off from a successful course. Students were pleased that the work was of interest to others and gratified that it was seen to have been of value. Art work is generally a rather solitary and private experience, but in this case the communication was direct and the feedback immediate.

The study not only helped the students understand the village, but also affected their subsequent work. Thus one student commented: 'I think this study can cause people to see an apparently familiar place in a completely different way, as if they had opened their eyes a bit wider and were able to understand reasons for it being like that, just by looking at it more carefully.' And another said: 'It has made me look much closer at the built environment of Portsmouth.'

On their return to school, students were asked to assess the experience in terms of the following questions:

- What did you think were the aims of the course?
- What did you think about the content of the course?
- What did you think about the organization of the work?
- Do you think you made a contribution to the course?
- How would you assess your overall effort?
- What do you think about this sort of study?
- What suggestions can you make for improvement?

The flavour of the course and the nature of the games
approach is best conveyed by the teacher's diary.

JULY
1979

FRIDAY
6
2.15 p.m. Minibuses and Landrover fully loaded with equipment, food, beds, suitcases, staff and students. Set off for Stoke St. Gregory. Three hour journey. Students asked to note variations, significant, subtle or blatant as we proceed through the countryside. On arrival, all equipment unloaded, village hall to be organised for eating, sleeping, working, meal to prepare, work rotas to be sorted out. Went like clockwork (the army have got nothing on us. 20.00: Introductory Talk: Eileen Adams, bombardment of vocabulary, working methods, examples of work 21.30: Retired for liquid refreshment.

SATURDAY
7
08.00: Breakfast not quite ready, students had managed to set the tables, but not actually make the breakfast! 09.00 Input by Eileen: explore the village, record, notate as much as possible, comment about, aim for 30 drawings. Do not be worried about 'good' drawings. Content much more important. 12.00 All work displayed. Students criticised for being too precious and self indulgent. Map to be drawn of area explored. 12.30 – 14.00 Lunch 14.00 Serial Vision 1: Move along a road, note changes in mass and space. Produce 6 drawings at 6 stopping points. Comment on changes, differences, contrast one with another, state preferred location. 16.00 Slide presentation

09.00 Serial Vision 2 A more controlled version of 1. Cut out view finder like 35 mm slide. Travel 100 yds stop each 15/20 paces. The scenery will be revealed in series of revelations. React to contrast. Take account of existing view, vanished view, emerging view. Develop a drawing or notation system which will convey this experience.
11.15 Sensory Walk. Map/diagram to be produced of places visited. Same area as Serial Vision 2 can be used. At each point, listen, taste, smell, touch, remember, see, wonder. Think of various/appropriate recording media.. 16.00: Diaries – bring up to date, make sure all is recorded, observations noted.. Evening: discussion on days work.

MONDAY
9
09.00 I. SPY: Vocabulary. Find and record the following, make comments on the quality: enclave, enclosure, focal point, visual block, defining space, change of level, silhouette, target, scale view, intimate view, projection and recession, penetration, rhythm, repetition, anticipation, mystery, detail, scale.
11.00. Locate and explore a building, or group of buildings ready for afternoon session. 11.30. A journey: recalled from memory six items noted en-route. Location Sedgemoor! – analyse in relation to work done in village. 14.00: Hide and Seek. Explore all angles, facets, viewpoints: relate to I. SPY: Pay attention to space viewed from and through. 19.00: Evening presentation and discussion

09.00 Snakes and Ladders: Two sets of work
in series. One set from top of church tower (120') out
set from the base. Both to be facing same direction. Start
by looking down at floor and work up in stages until the
horizon is reached. Use a viewfinder. Make comment on major
differences in each set of work. Record the journey to the top of
the tower. State why your particular direction chosen.

14.00 Tiddleywinks: Use viewfinder to zoom in on one of the
details noticeable in the far distance. Always keep this detail in
view. Approach detail and stop at various points, record not just
changes in space or shape but pay particular attention to 'depth of field'
as in a photograph. Delineation will constantly change.

09.00 Skittles 1. Find a panoramic view, not too vast, and draw it.
2. Explore the area just drawn by walking into it. What is hidden
3. Record as much as possible before moving again into the area
still hidden. 4. Produce 9 drawings of space/area moved through.
5. Working in the studio and again on location if need be
produce a series of drawings which show the significant changes
that occur as each group of objects is removed. Make comments
on these changes, which is liked or disliked. Why?

14.00 Using the view from the vicarage garden, reverse the morning
session - add to the view either cultivated or constructed items.
Give reasons for decisions.

09.00. Uppers and Downers. Produce two sets or
series of drawings, fully notated. 1. High - the area or group of
buildings which you find the most interesting and stimulating.
2. Low - the area or building or group of buildings which is the
most depressing, decayed/disliked restored etc. Try to evaluate the
differences in whatever way seems appropriate.

14.00. L.S.D. Produce two contrasting studies which show in your
opinion the difference between a poor and an expensive area. Be
aware that there might be very different reasons for choice in
relation to Uppers and Downers. Try and note these differences.

09.00 Monopoly - Group activity. Four groups. Four rounds
north, south, east, west; Each group to record facades of buildings
and spaces and place some value on each site. Reasons to be
clearly stated in drawing. Work to be mounted in sequence.
.00 Discussion based on mornings work.
.00 Pass the Parcel. 1. Draw a building 2. Pass on to somebody
+ 3. Trace it and then make additions or alterations. 4. Pass
the tracing. 5. Continue process. 6. Assemble work into sequence
/ assess the development of original building.
0 - Pack up and go home.

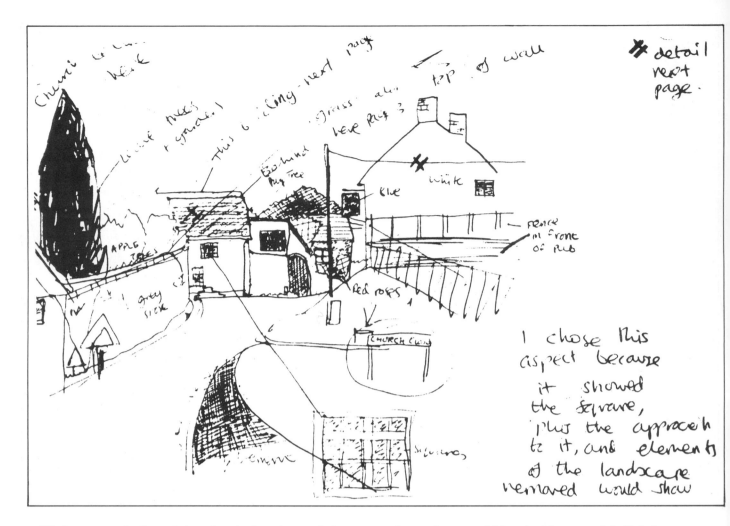

Their answers indicated that they had understood the critical bias of the study and were very conscious of the emphasis on developing recording skills: 'to sharpen our observation and teach us to draw rigorously'; 'to help us understand our environment and be able to say what we like and dislike about it and to be able to give reasons for our opinions.'

They felt that the course had been demanding, but that the variety of drawing exercises and study tasks sustained a high level of interest. Students were not used to the fast working techniques demanded and had previously tended to adopt only one drawing style. The experience of a number of alternative approaches, each with its own particular value, offered new possibilities: 'The course included a variety of different ways of looking at the environment and I found this very interesting and also helpful as it made me see things in a completely new light.'

After the initial stimulus, the teachers assessed the work at the end of each day in order to decide the best way to proceed. Although a framework for study had been agreed, no definite plan had been arranged, so that the study should relate to the students' needs and capacities, the place and the weather. This could be misinterpreted by the students — 'I think it was a good idea that the teachers did not know anything about the work until the very day, as it seemed to put them more in the picture and able to discuss things better with us', or 'On the whole the organization was very good considering that the organizers were unsure what they were doing from day to day.'

Students recognized that the discussion and sharing of experience and ideas had been useful: 'I feel everyone made a contribution by producing work and ideas which others could use.' Some tended to view the value of their contribution in relation to the thickness of their folder of work: 'I think we all must have made some contribution since we all produced a large folder by the end of the week.' But it was not equally easy for everyone. 'I extracted as much as I was able from the work, but I don't feel I was able to give much in return. I had plenty of good ideas in my head but I found I was unable to put them on paper. They were more feelings than actual things to write down.'

Some were also very frank about their assessment of their own work: 'I was often tempted to draw something visually appealing rather than what I actually saw or felt about it, and put in too much detail that interested me — indulged far too much'. And others were disarmingly frank: 'I can honestly say that I worked harder during that one week in Somerset than I have ever worked in any subject, particularly art'; 'I found this course very tough, but I worked hard and feel that I have achieved a lot for myself.'

Probably because the study had been an enjoyable one, students tended to view the Project work favourably. 'I feel this type of study is original and thus interesting and successful. The intensity of the work is an experience in itself. Relating art to the built environment helps connect the work we do with our lives and surroundings and widens our knowledge of the subject. Art no longer becomes another school subject, but a part of everyday existence', and 'I think this type of study is very, very important. Because it

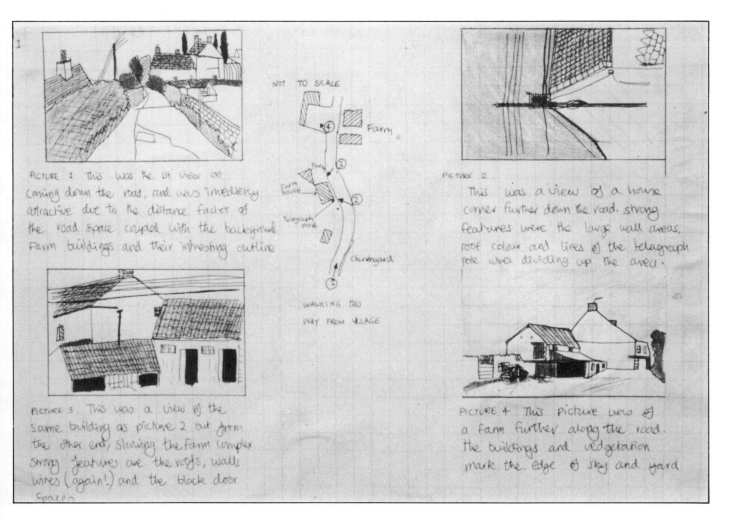

PICTURE 1 This was the 1st view on coming down the road, and was immediately attractive due to the distance factor of the road space coupled with the background Farm buildings and their interesting outline

PICTURE 2. This was a view of a house corner further down the road, strong features were the large wall areas, roof colour and lines of the telegraph pole wires dividing up the area.

PICTURE 3. This was a view of the same building as picture 2 but from the other end, showing the Farm complex. Strong features are the roofs, walls wires (again!) and the black door spaces.

PICTURE 4 This picture was of a farm further along the road. the buildings and vegetation mark the edge of sky and yard

not only helps us understand art more deeply, but it helps us understand ourselves, the things around us and the effect they have on us.'

In their suggestions for improving the course, students recommended more discussion and a change of activity in the final working session in the evening. Teachers tended to advise students individually about their work, but the students gained a lot from group 'crit. sessions' and discussions about ways of working. 'I feel that the evening session should have been kept not for any new topics but left as a time when the day's work could be collected together, organized and discussed, to give time for the group to sort out ideas and then start the next day afresh. I found myself still thinking about the last day's work.' By comparison with their study of Portsmouth the field trip seemed to have given more. 'We should either have gone to Somerset before we did the study of Portsmouth, or we should have had the aim explained. We had just been left to draw what we wanted so the work from Portsmouth bore no relation to that in Somerset.' 'It would have been an idea to have a week set aside for similar intensive work in Portsmouth, but this seems difficult because of time. We now know much more of what is needed, therefore the Portsmouth work now seems worthless.' Several other students echoed this view.

change your environment

street road avenue lane path
alley arcade mall grove way walk
promenade esplanade boulevard
expressway motorway
terrace circus crescent
square block row
hamlet estate town
neighbourhood village
city suburb new town
slum general improvement
area housing action area
conurbation province
metropolis resort camp
cafe pub restaurant
teashop coffeeshop bar
snack bar canteen bistro
newsagent fruitshop grocer's
butcher's baker's library
police station railway station
office bank post office
laundrette off licence
cornershop estate agent's
solicitor's betting shop
funeral parlour cobbler's
hairdresser's building site
demolition area hotel
supermarket flower stall
stationer's confectioner's
town hall church
school hospital factory
tower block warehouse
garden yard brewery
leisure centre swimming pool
park beach cinema theatre
bingo hall chemist's
furniture shop market
building society precinct
fire station bus station

flat
duplex
cottage hall chalet
priory rectory
tent maisonette
caravan house grange
attic digs
residence guest house
hostel penthouse prison
har
flatlet apartment
cabin lodge
shanty garret motel
terrace cellar
mews town hou
semi basement farm
bungalow
villa

116

14 General studies courses

It is our impression that sixth form general studies courses are usually dominated by sociology, current affairs, personal relations and similar topics. There are several well-known thematic guides to an educationally justifiable general studies course, but this particular slot in the timetable tends to be a last resort for squeezing in all those topics which managed to get left out of the curriculum in previous years, or else a mere rag-bag of unrelated items where individual teachers may show a willingness to promote a particular interest. There is much to be said for promoting classroom discussion on general themes as an aspect of the students' personal development, but a general studies programme based on sins of omission or personal whim is scarcely a sound basis for education.

The schools' casual attitude and the low status of non-examination subjects are reflected in poor commitment, poor motivation and poor attendance. This is in striking contrast to some of our trial schools which had formulated a positive general studies policy, and where students were encouraged to see these studies, not as peripheral or optional, but as an important aspect of their general education.

Another cause for concern is the poor provision for the development of discriminatory and critical capacities. Our experience has indicated that very little attention is given to this aspect of students' educational development, even in areas like English, which includes criticism in its area of responsibility. There is, all too often, a token acknowledgement of the necessity to promote critical skills but this is interpreted as reading what the critics say, with the constant need to refer to established academic authorities.

The most successful *Art and the Built Environment* courses have usually been in schools where general studies as a whole are seen as a positive and valuable means of broadening the students' educational experience. Adequate provision is made for general studies, not as an afterthought or a way of filling up the students' day, but as an important and integral part of the curriculum. Here the onus is not only on the teachers to make a strong case for their particular contribution, but on curriculum planners to recognize the possibilities and plan accordingly.

Some of the most interesting *Art and the Built Environment* courses have developed in sixth form general studies programmes which provide an excellent opportunity for art teachers to contribute in the context of general education. In the sixth form general studies course the tendency has been for art teachers, when involved, to concentrate on the historical/cultural domain, mainly through the history of art or architecture. The analytical/critical domain is poorly acknowledged, with perhaps the odd gesture to consumer education through comparative studies of products. However, the art appreciation course, with slides from the teacher's Italian holiday, or the design course based on the Sunday Colour Supplements and a visit to the Design Centre, are hardly the best way of exploiting the role of art in general education. Neither is the 'art for leisure' course, where art is seen as therapy or as an escape from other more demanding activities.

Some teachers in our Project have found that in the development of a critical language students may be more forthcoming in the general studies class than in the art class. A-level Art students are inclined to say that the image speaks for itself, whereas general studies students are not so arrogant and endeavour to make their meaning explicit.

In preparing courses, much of the teachers' concern has been with the nature of critical response and the kinds of learning activities which might elicit this. Teachers have considered the following questions, and have sought to develop appropriate courses for a wide range of students:

> **Experience**
> What are the possibilities for environmental study? What are the appropriate activities that will encourage a heightened subjective, affective response?
> **Appraisal**
> What study methods may be used both in the street and in the classroom which might develop or refine that response, and so promote perceptual development?
> **Criticism**
> What vocabulary and skills will develop powers of discrimination and criticism?
> **Expression**
> How might students communicate their critical response to townscape?

Sheredes School, Hoddesdon

At Sheredes School at Hoddesdon in Hertfordshire, the general studies course is called Central Studies and comprises 3 double periods a week for all the students in the first year sixth. This is part of the school's policy related to a core curriculum, where certain areas of study are considered important for everyone — not just those students who think they might be interested in them, or for students who want to opt out of something else, as is so often the case when students are presented with a range of options.

Art and the Built Environment work in this Central Studies course is a 6 week unit, one of several allocated to general studies topics with the theme of 'Man in Society'. A team of teachers from different subject disciplines is responsible for devising and instituting the course. This meant that in the *Art and the Built Environment* unit teachers had an opportunity to work with other members of staff from other disciplines.

All first year sixth form students had previously followed a 5 year course of art and design, and all had taken a CSE examination in this subject. Some were continuing their studies in art at A–level, while others had chosen different subjects for examination.

The students' previous art experience (another aspect of the core curriculum philosophy of this school) provided a sound basis for the work. They were familiar with visual/tactile modes of study and had developed a good range of skills in handling a wide variety of media. They possessed a degree of confidence and competence which enabled us to concentrate more on the ideas concerning critical appraisal than on the manipulation of expressive media.

During a 3 year period Sheredes School cooperated with the Project team in developing a course each year. The first half of the summer term was selected as the best time, when the weather was good for streetwork and when more staff were available as the fifth year was involved in examinations. Some of the art staff used their preparation periods to work on the Project.

The courses at Sheredes sought to promote the 2 basic Project aims of encouraging greater environmental awareness and developing discriminatory and critical skills in relation to the built environment. The programme differed each year, each successive course being modified by the experience of the previous year. There were also some staff changes, and naturally those teachers with a continuing commitment to the work developed an increasing confidence and capability in helping the students.

We give here an account of the first and the last studies. Both were concerned with a central area in a small town. The Hatfield study demonstrates the school's first attempt to tackle this kind of project and the Hertford study explains how the teachers progressed towards developing appropriate skills and study techniques to cope adequately with the demands of a critical appraisal.

The Hatfield Study

Aims: To develop greater awareness; to develop discriminatory and critical skills in relation to the built environment.

Planning: Having agreed to include an *Art and the Built Environment* course within the Central Studies programme, the art department, in cooperation with the other members of the Central Studies team, set about planning a course which would fit in with the general context of the Central Studies programme and would also relate to the demands of the Project. The planning meetings revealed a sympathy of aims and working methods between the teachers and the Project Team and gave everyone a chance to familiarize themselves with the Project ideas. It was also necessary to work out ideas and practical details of organization such as staffing, working space, activities and materials. There was much discussion about the range and type of study methods which might be appropriate. We hoped the students would explore the sensory qualities of the study areas and attempt some assessment of different places. We were interested in providing opportunities to explore, discover and investigate; how we could enlarge students' receptivity to new experience, new ideas, how we might record these; how they might be developed and communicated. We prepared a study booklet for the students as a support, and as reference, containing maps, the proposed time table

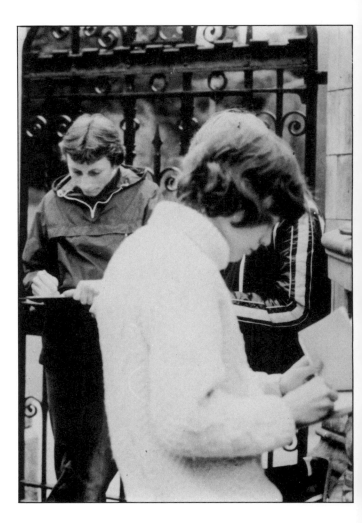

of the course, the background to the Project, ideas for the study and Keith Wheeler's townscape notation system.

The basis for the course was direct experience of townscape and the streetwork was one of the most important aspects of the study. We were anxious that this should provide as rich an experience as possible, but at first were uncertain of the best way to encourage an enlarged and deepened response. It was decided to use the local area of Hoddesdon in a first study to test out possible approaches and students' responses, and then to build on that experience with another study, of Hatfield, 15 miles away.

Introduction: The sensory walk provided a useful introduction to the study. The necessity to look afresh at a familiar environment and experience it at a different level introduced the students to a particular important approach and to the need to rely on their own personal perceptions. Ideas and information were recorded through drawing, writing and photography. Students worked in groups, each exploring a different route near the school. In each group there were at least 1 or 2 A-level Art students, so that those who were not very skilful in visual study or presentation had the security of a working group, and each student could make a specific contribution from a range of possible choices. Students were asked to communicate their response through a presentation of any visual material that described their experience. A series of display panels was set up at the end of the 2 week study, and a 'crit. session' held to discuss the work. The trails which evolved were presented through photographs, drawings, maps, diagrams and written explanation. Each group prepared a panel, 8 feet by 4 feet, so that the work could be easily viewed and discussed. The standard both of content and presentation was good, and reflected the students' previous experience in their CSE Art course which stressed the importance of visual language both in terms of understanding and communicating ideas. Notions of sensory experience, emotional response and visual communication were discussed. The exhibition/'crit. session' gave students an opportunity to compare their work with that of the others, gave a sense of achievement and was a stimulus for further effort.

The studios were available for 2 double periods, and, in the Hatfield study, we also had another single period which was used for seminars, lectures and exhibitions. This provided an invaluable opportunity to stand back and consider the work in progress, or to introduce a different kind of input, and made for a greater understanding of the practical work.

These sessions were organized by different members of staff giving lectures or presenting exhibitions. These included slide presentations on ideas for study, serial vision and visual communication. This last was set in an exhibition of original art works based on environmental–reference. These were borrowed from the County collection and offered an excellent setting for a comparison of the artist's view with that of the critic. A local architect was invited to present his views on townscape and the constraints of the architect — 2 sessions that proved to be provocative as well as informative. Other people had the opportunity to present their ideas and perceptions as a way of helping students focus and define their own.

Streetwork at Hatfield: The students approached the Hatfield study less tentatively than before and were more aware of the possibilities for study. They seemed more confident and more prepared to encounter different kinds of sensory experience. Hatfield, a new town with an old core, was chosen as the major study area. Half the group explored the new shopping centre, and the other half the rehabilitated older part of the town. They were asked to investigate their area and to make a statement about their visit, to explain what kind of place it was, and what their response had been. They were asked in fact to assess the spirit of the place.

The school bus was used to ferry the group to and from the area and the journey was used as a last briefing session. Teachers worked with the groups and were available to encourage and support students during the streetwork which included recording the material through drawings, photography, writing and tape recording.
Studio work: While most of the students made a good start, a number gradually moved away from their original ideas for a variety of reasons — wrong choice of materials, lack of craft expertise or inappropriate scale. Surprisingly few used painting as a medium. Collage, both 2- and 3-dimensional, was a most popular form or expression. So too was clay, though for some their aspirations did not match their expertise. Photographs were a basic working medium for many: Instamatic colour prints formed the basis of one well-designed board game. Material surfaces and textures were reflected in a number of works, from a piece of weaving by one girl at her own loom, to a large relief of floorscape by another. 2 students produced 8-minute colour films, one with commentary, the other with a music sound track. Two others created an abstract sound tape, edited from recorded sounds at Hatfield and other found sounds.

Like all other creative experiences, whether group or individual, the final weeks of the studio work had their troughs as well as their high points. The commitment to a final exhibition of work helped to maintain a healthy level of tension and involvement, and the experience of the exhibition itself proved to be very exciting and worthwhile, as it showed the value and importance of individual contributions, and made it clear that a group of people might have a shared experience or might be exposed to the same stimuli, yet have very different perceptions of it, learn different things and understand ideas in different ways. The result was not to suggest that one response or approach is more valid than another, it was to illustrate the fact that personal, honest responses and understanding are as diverse as the people themselves, and that it is important that we should have our own opinions and make our own decisions, and should be prepared to explain and justify them.

The students all expressed their ideas through some form of visual imagery, which was evidence of their personal and emotional response, though it did not constitute a full critical appraisal. However, at that particular phase of the Project, it was helpful in that the work showed the relevance of art as part of everyone's educational experience. The students' confidence in attempting the study and their willingness to experiment reflected their previous experience and the school's philosophy that art is a basic and necessary study for all its pupils. The staff were surprised and pleased at the level of commitment and degree of involvement that was achieved. The students felt that working in groups on the sensory walk had been the easier part of the work, and that the open nature of the second assignment was more difficult but more rewarding.

The Hertford Study

The final ABE course at Sheredes School during the Project's 3 year research period aimed to develop work primarily concerned with the development of critical skills in relation to a study of the built environment, and evolved from the experience of the 2 previous courses at the school. The art staff felt that this work had successfully encouraged an

enlarged personal, emotional response to townscape, but had not necessarily demonstrated a critical response.

Because of the limited time available for the research, this course was held in the autumn term. It lasted for 2 (1 hour 10 minutes) lessons for 10 weeks. Our experience at Sheredes suggests that the best time for streetwork is early in the autumn term or after Easter.

Some of the art teachers had been involved in the previous studies, and assumed that the other teachers involved understood the aims and possible directions of the study. However, the newcomers were at first uncertain of their role and how they could best promote the work. Meetings were held before, during and after the course for staff to consider ideas for study and consider suitable learning activities; to monitor the development of the work; and to assess this in order to determine possibilities for the future. Teachers are continually assessing their work and making plans, but it is even more vital for a team of teachers to work together on curriculum development, where each can draw support from others' enthusiasm and judgement. A mixed team of teachers, including history, geography and drama, joined members of the art department in the study. It was useful to have a drama teacher involved, as comparisons could be made of criticism in the context of art, drama and townscape. Discussion at staff meetings during the course was primarily concerned with what might constitute a critical response and what were the most appropriate ways to communicate this in the context of *Art and the Built Environment* work. All students in the first year sixth Central Studies programme were involved. Of the 46 students, 10 had chosen to do A-level Art. Each of the 3 groups who had been involved in ABE work at Sheredes seemed to be different in character, and, although a course framework was prepared at the beginning of each study, this had to be modified and adapted to suit the needs of the particular students involved.

The course was based on a study of 2 different areas: the local area in Hoddesdon, where 6 routes were selected for an introduction to streetwork; and Hertford, the small county town some miles away which was the main study area.

During the earlier *Art and the Built Environment* work at Sheredes, we had found a study booklet very helpful for the students. From this we had developed an issue of the *Bulletin of Environmental Education* for general use as a students' briefing. The Project was introduced through this at Sheredes and elsewhere in the final year of our work.

Study areas were selected by teachers on the basis of variety, distance from school and length of route. In a suburban residential community like Hoddesdon, there is a range of different types of housing, which offered a basis for comparison. But because of time limits, we could not choose areas very far from the school, as that would have cut down on time available for study. It was also advisable to have students working in small groups in a number of different places rather than a large number together, so students were sent off in different directions to work in groups of around 6 under the direction of a teacher. The sixth form staffing ratio is not usually so generous, but members of the art department had again forfeited preparatory periods to join in the study.

The idea was to involve the students in streetwork as soon as possible, so a preliminary exploration was introduced in the second lesson. After discussion of their experience, this was followed by another session to record particular information about the townscape qualities of the various study areas. It was assumed that specific study skills would be learnt during the course of the work, but later, teachers felt that perhaps more time should have been given at the beginning of the course to ensure that students understood properly the expectations and demands of the course, and were more prepared to cope with them.

There was no particular budget for this course, and materials used were very simple — paper and 6 rolls of black and white film, processing and some printing. To cut down on expense, each of the 6 groups were allowed only one 20 exposure roll of film to record their route. A photographer — either a student or a teacher — was appointed in each group, and all members selected a series of shots which best explained the character of the study area. Contact sheets were made, and groups could choose up to 6 photographs for printing. Any other illustration on their presentations had to be provided through drawings, diagrams or maps. Many of the groups used paper collage to explain their route.

However, although each display was relatively successful in communicating the content of the route and was an excellent way of providing description, they did not necessarily convey a critical response. This was more evident during the groups' presentations, when students were asked to explain their choices and justify their opinions. This gave an opportunity for value judgements to be discussed and evaluated and perceptions compared. At this point, there was much discussion among the staff about what might constitute a critical response. At first it was thought this could be communicated purely through visual means, but it became evident that criticism demanded more than the development of descriptive skills. The emphasis had been on interpreting and communicating sensory experience, but criticism demanded the use of verbal or written explanation to clarify or justify judgements. It was not sufficient that they might be implicit in the selection and arrangement of the visual display; they had to be made explicit through the use of words, so there could be no doubt what meaning was intended.

Once again, the students approached the second study more confidently than their initial work at Hoddesdon, as they were more aware of the kind of information that was required and felt better prepared for the task. However, teachers were not satisfied that students had developed an adequate critical vocabulary, so a study session was given to an explanation and discussion of appropriate words, ways of describing townscape qualities, ways of communicating a critical response. A list of words was considered, which was intended as reference during the study, and certain townscape features which students might encounter, discussed, such as new buildings in old settings, rehabilitation or personalization. This last topic led to a heated discussion about the freedom of the individual versus community interest, and debate on planning and participation processes. None of the students had known that decisions about their environment were made by local councillors on their behalf, and that they would have a right to influence those decisions.

Arrangements were made to have an extra lesson for the streetwork session at Hertford, so that with journey time of $\frac{1}{4}$ hour each way, this left $1\frac{1}{2}$ hours for study. The main briefing concerning the purpose and expectations of the lesson had been explained in the previous session — unfortunately, 10 days before, because of the intervening half term. Therefore the main points were repeated on the school bus, and study sheets distributed: study brief, place assessment sheet, vocabulary sheets, together with clipboards and paper. It had been decided to use annotated sketches rather than photography to record information on this session as it was felt that drawing encouraged greater observation and concentration, and, if tackled properly, would focus and direct looking, and enable students to see, understand and appreciate more fully their study subject. Students were asked to make a detailed description of their study site, using drawings and words, and to appraise it critically, stating personal opinions, giving reasons for their judgements.

Students worked in the small study groups, each taking a different section of the town centre. Individuals were then allocated specific study sites. Where only one building was specified, there was a tendency to view it in isolation, without reference to the context of the rest of the streetscape. Comments were generally related to individual building elements, rather than the building as a whole in relation to the space in which it stood; in fact, spatial qualities were not well documented and detail was given more importance than total impact in many cases. Written notes tended to repeat drawn information. These were all responses that we observed in other schools too.

Those students who had recorded a lot of information in detail found it easier to develop their studies than those whose work demonstrated a more superficial response. The immediate follow-up to the streetwork is one of the most difficult parts of this type of study, when information has to be collated, interpreted, analysed, developed, refined, and decisions made as to how to communicate the experience, and the thoughts, ideas and opinions it generated. The staff agreed there was a need for greater emphasis on observational study, drawing skills and perhaps a slower working pace to make sure that previous learning experiences had been assimilated.

The reason I chose this view was, that I thought that the actual view was aesthetically inter-esting and would have been very intim-ate and cosy but for the wideness of the road. I feel this is distinctive to the overall image. This leaves the eyes being assaulted by a monotonous blandness which is uncharacter-istic for the style of buildings.

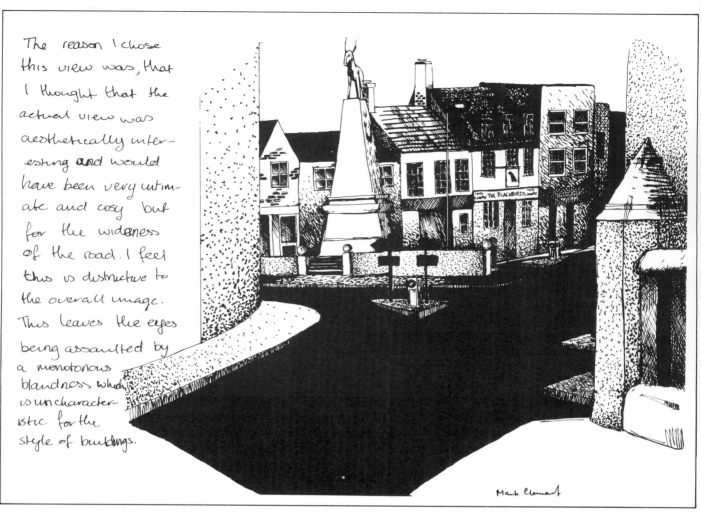

Mark Clement

SHAUN PICKERING

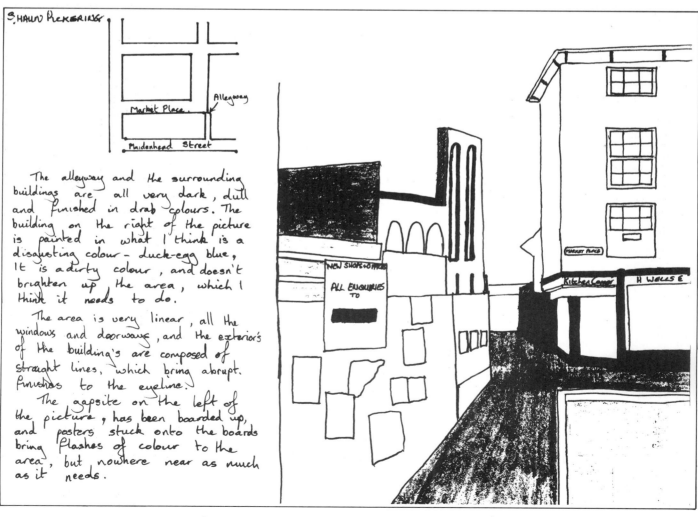

Market Place   Allegway
Maidenhead Street

The alleyway and the surrounding buildings are all very dark, dull and finished in drab colours. The building on the right of the picture is painted in what I think is a disgusting colour - duck-egg blue, It is a dirty colour, and doesn't brighten up, the area, which I think it needs to do.

The area is very linear, all the windows and doorways, and the exteriors of the building's are composed of straight lines, which bring abrupt finishes to the eyeline.

The gapsite on the left of the picture, has been boarded up, and posters stuck onto the boards bring flashes of colour to the area, but nowhere near as much as it needs.

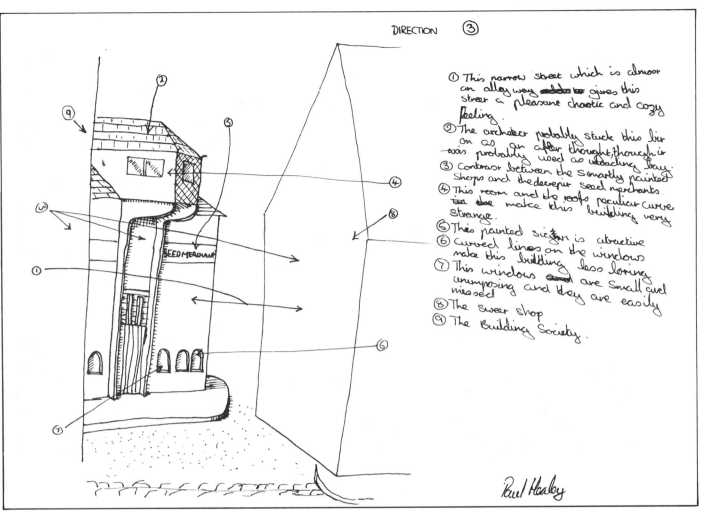

DIRECTION ③

① This narrow street which is almost an alley way ~~adds to~~ gives this street a pleasant chaotic and cozy feeling.

② The architect probably stuck this bit on as an after thought, though it was probably used as ~~attaching~~ they.

③ Contrast between the smartly painted shops and the decrepit seed merchants.

④ This room and the roofs peculiar curve ~~to the~~ make this building very strange.

⑤ This painted sign is attractive

⑥ Curved lines on the windows make this building less boring

⑦ This windows ~~and~~ are small and unimposing and they are easily missed

⑧ The sweet shop

⑨ The Building Society.

Paul Healey

MAIDENHEAD STREET

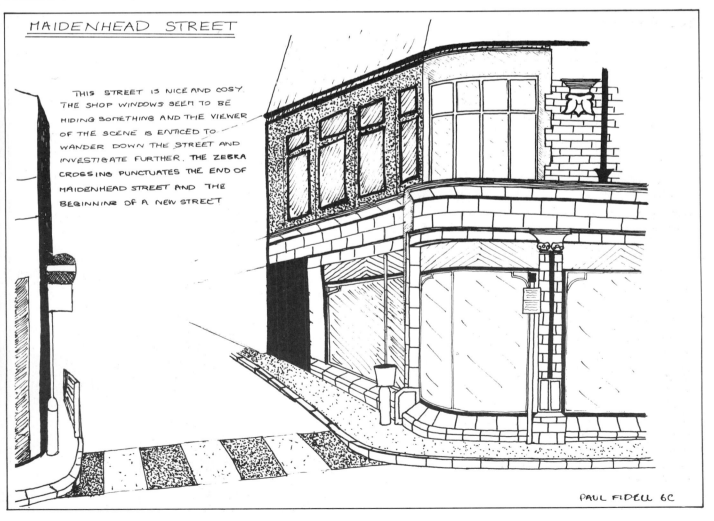

THIS STREET IS NICE AND COSY. THE SHOP WINDOWS SEEM TO BE HIDING SOMETHING AND THE VIEWER OF THE SCENE IS ENTICED TO WANDER DOWN THE STREET AND INVESTIGATE FURTHER. THE ZEBRA CROSSING PUNCTUATES THE END OF MAIDENHEAD STREET AND THE BEGINNING OF A NEW STREET

PAUL FIDELL 6C

The teacher's role here is crucial — to stimulate and direct discussion and argument, and to support further study. One teacher investigated more fully than others his students' understanding of the vocabulary which had been used throughout the study, and found they had not fully grasped the meaning of many of the terms teachers had taken for granted would be generally understood. Or even if they knew what was meant, some students could not necessarily recognize particular townscape qualities. For instance the word 'progression' was not understood as a series, but as a reference to a new building in an old setting. Words like 'scale' and 'rhythm' were considered relevant to music rather than to townscape.

Students in these groups were typical of the 16 year olds throughout the study, whose critical vocabulary was generally much more limited than teachers had imagined. It was not until students had gained some confidence in working together that they were prepared to ask questions about ideas or terminology they did not understand. Working in small study groups helped students establish working relationships with one another and provided welcome support for individual studies. Teachers came to know a few people quite well, and were therefore able to offer appropriate support and encouragement.

Streetwork

Skills

Peter Symonds College

It was decided to include *Art and the Built Environment* work in the general studies programme at Peter Symonds College, offering it as a creative arts choice, as well as integrating it with the A-level Art course. This made the work available to a wider range of students, all of whom could choose a non-examination course for ½ day a week in the first year of the sixth form course. The original intention was to establish the work within the art department, then to involve a wider range of subject disciplines. For 2 years a geography teacher has worked with an art teacher to develop the course. The following account explains the course that has evolved from their cooperation.

During the first attempt to devise a course for general studies several approaches and areas of work were attempted. A study of a semi-derelict street due for demolition produced work based on people, materials, textures and contrasts, but did not offer sufficient stimulus to maintain interest for more than a term. Students lacked the basic visual skills and thus had no confidence in tackling visual appraisal. They were reluctant to draw, preferring the comparative security of a camera or tape recorder, though they were not always sure what to make of their information once they had recorded it. Perhaps they developed a greater capacity to express opinions verbally, but they could offer little evidence of how they had arrived at these judgements. At first members of staff were also reluctant to impose their own perceptions or working methods, which meant that students did not receive enough support to devise and develop their own personal studies. As with the A-level Art group, they had no model on which to develop an art based environmental study.

Tutorial

One of the major aims of the current course has been to learn from this experience and approach the work in a different way. The teachers later agreed that there is a difference between imposing one's own views on students and providing study methods whereby students can be encouraged to think for themselves. Study methods have been made more explicit and the emphasis has been on coming to terms with the problems of environmental study of this kind.

Study skills were more clearly defined and specific demands made on students, which became increasingly complex as students gained more familiarity and confidence in handling ideas and experiences. Drawing skills were considered central to the work and the value of annotated sketches was stressed; the need for economic, particular, specific statements, rather than superficially attractive drawings, was emphasized.

The course aimed to vary both the study environments and the learning activities and to create an appropriate balance between streetwork and classwork. It was decided that the school campus should be used initially, and then the neighbouring streets and a central area of the town, before organizing comparative studies in other places. Consideration was given to the students' lack of experience of this kind of work, to the time, resources and transport available. A draft programme was prepared which could be modified if the need arose.

The study was introduced by a slide presentation describing various possibilities for townscape study which led to a discussion on perception and the importance of emotional response. Students were sent on an exploration of the campus, based on a series of photographs taken by a member of the A-level Art group. These recorded a number of familiar locations photographed from unusual angles or isolated from their particular context, and

students, working in pairs, were required to explore the campus, identify the locations and record them through annotated sketches. This led to further identification and description of the various areas which demonstrated particular townscape qualities: seclusion, invitation, calm, excitement, anticipation, surprise, public and private space. Students were required to consider how buildings formed particular qualities of space both inside and out, so that in the first lesson they needed to make aesthetic judgements. This first exercise proved a useful diagnostic tool for the teachers, to find out what degree of understanding students had reached, and it also served to introduce the students to each other. The variety of activities — looking at slides, listening, commenting, discussing, exploring, observing, and drawing — encouraged a good level of interest and involvement.

In the first few weeks exercises in drawing, tape recording, still and cine photography were set up in relation to environmental exploration, to provide students with the means of recording different kinds of information and to give them confidence in handling different types of

Studio work

Crit. session

Peter Symonds college
Creative studies programme
"Art and the built environment" option.

Draft programme

Autumn Term:
aim – to develop discriminatory and critical
skills in relation to townscape study.

1	introduction streetwork	'Townscape' – a critical study campus – photo quiz	slide programme exploration observation sketchbooks
2	streetwork	campus – identification of aesthetic qualities	recording information through drawing
3	streetwork	campus – viewpoints	recording/communicating information through photography
	(optional:	photographic workshop	processing techniques)
4	studio	presentation of work crit. session briefing session for next week's work	reporting discussion
	(optional:	lecture: 'The architect's view.')	
5	streetwork	local area	critical appraisal
6	studio	presentation of work	reporting
7	studio	visual communication	ways of ordering and presenting information
8	studio streetwork	introduction to central area study initial exploration	observation
9			
10			
11	streetwork/ studio work	central area study	
12	as necessary		
13			
14	studio	presentations of central area studies	

Spring Term:
aim – to promote discriminatory skills through the ability
to make comparisons.
Compare Winchester central area with that of another town.
Compare different viewpoints of various people about townscape:
e.g. architect, engineer, artist, photographer, resident.
Simulation – (cooperate with drama group) – based on viewpoints.

Summer Term: To prepare trails based on critical appraisal of townscape –
e.g. village trail: Alternative Winchester trail.

media. For instance, one exercise based on the exploration of the campus gave students 50 minutes to choose a number of sites to be recorded on the basis of visual attraction or repulsion. It was found that places to which they felt indifferent were rather more difficult to analyse. Work was displayed and discussed. It demonstrated a wide range of perceptions — some students chose the same sites but responded differently to them.

A further exercise was based on 'serial vision' — the experience of space as we move through it and the changes in our perceptions as we move. The notion of viewpoint took on a particular importance here, and cameras were used to compare different viewpoints, both physical and intellectual. Students were asked to select and record particular sites of their choice and to use up to 10 shots to record them, attempting to find viewpoints that would successfully convey their feelings about the place. They were thus introduced, early in the work, to the tasks of selecting, recording, interpreting, informing themselves and communicating feelings and ideas.

The next study was of 2 nearby streets. The students were asked to select 2 points: the line between them was to be their focus for study, looking at the inside and outside, public and private spaces, front and rear, to present their appraisal of a restricted segment of townscape. Study methods were to be similar to those used on the campus. But students tended to concentrate on the facades, and did not investigate the back lanes or gardens adequately enough to provide a full picture of the place. The need to prepare an explanation of their response and to present their ideas and opinions to the rest of the group was a useful exercise, as some problems were identified that would have to be considered in the next stage of the study. A number of students had difficulty in identifying aesthetic qualities; most of them tended to take a limited range of viewpoints to observe their study subject, and had recorded insufficient information to describe the study area satisfactorily.

The major project of the first term was a study of a central part of the town, comprising 2 shopping streets together with a number of side streets and back lanes: commercial and residential development built up over several centuries. From the start this exploration seemed an exciting prospect, as students felt prepared and confident to tackle it, and a start was made with the students to determine how it should be approached in individual or small group studies. The vantage point of the multi-storey car park was used to consider the whole study area, and the possibilities were identified as the group walked through the town.

A room was reserved at the public library in case a work-base nearer the study area was needed. Teachers supervised the work through meetings with individuals and with tutorial sessions in the street as well as back in the college.

In a situation where there was a variety of choices, both of study subjects and of study methods, some students found it difficult to make an appropriate selection. Perhaps they felt obliged to cover the whole area, as they seemed to concentrate on themes, rather than on a particular small location within the study area. However, these themes tended to develop into mere labelling exercises rather than critical essays. For instance, studies of decoration or of shop-fronts identified and categorized various visual and physical qualities, but did not necessarily consider them in the context of the rest of the street, or their contribution to or detraction from the townscape as a whole. They did not necessarily demonstrate personal opinion or explain personal preferences. Studies like the usual ones of traffic flow proved too daunting for this kind of study: students became too engrossed in counting cars and recording information, but could make no sense of their findings in interpreting the car's effect on the townscape. Many of the studies relied too much on photography rather than on annotated sketches, though teachers felt that the more demanding activity of drawing and writing obliged students to think more carefully about the subject matter of their work.

The most successful studies were those in which students quickly focussed on their subject, and decided what evidence they needed to describe it, explain their response and find ways of recording the necessary information. The most effective of these were in fact presented through annotated sketches. The teachers felt that these were the key to learning how to come to terms with the appraisal of the environment: 'The value of direct personal visual statement, supported by written comment, is central to the work, and the use of other media must only be seen as a way of extending and enlarging that direct statement.' The students' journals were also an excellent way of checking the progress of the work.

There was, of course, a difference between the evidence in the sketchbooks and that prepared for group presentation. Initial steps might make sense only to the individual student, whereas the presentations were expected to communicate to the whole group. This is more than a merely neat presentation, because it involved testing out material on students with no involvement in the Project. It might also involve refining or exaggerating aspects of the information and ideas gathered, though of course this is bound to modify the freshness and power of the initial response. The essence of communication in the context of critical appraisal seems to hinge on the effective use of a combination of written and visual language, presented in an unambiguous way.

The studio sessions provided an opportunity for the group to meet and compare notes. Students involved in the A-level Art course were happy to help colleagues with the presentation of their work, though all of them had to struggle with the problem of developing a critical vocabulary.

The need to communicate involved students in both expression and interpretation. Ideas that were considered self-evident to the originator were not accessible to others unless they could read the particular language used. It is here that the teacher should intervene to help students with a critical assessment of their own work and to suggest specific techniques to improve it.

As in several other *Art and the Built Environment* studies, students were asked to comment on the course:

'My knowledge of the various aspects of art was limited, and I wanted to broaden my outlook. *Art and the Built Environment* seemed an ideal opportunity to do this, so I opted for the course. It did not turn out quite as I expected, but I still enjoyed it. I had visions of the group studying just the more important buildings of Winchester, and perhaps the surrounding areas. I was pleasantly surprised with our study areas. There were 2 types of Wednesday afternoon — those working in our study area and those doing studio work. We would have a study brief, then we would disperse and work on our own particular aspects of the course. We would then return to base and discuss the work, the problems etc. I think it would have been beneficial to hear other people talk about the built environment who were not connected with the actual course, like landscape architects and town planners. The course made me more observant, giving me a greater understanding of buildings, and it has also taught me how to express my views.' HELEN FITTON

'The course had a free and easy atmosphere which, after 5 years of strictly controlled lessons, was a new experience and helped release reactions to buildings. A number of us had never used equipment such as cameras, tape recorders and cine before, and it opened up new channels for looking at the environment around us. The main difference was the freedom allowed by course tutors, and the fact that we were allowed to have a say in what we did, the course relying a great deal on the contribution of group members for its success. The best afternoons were spent away from Winchester in other environments which were unfamiliar and held more interest: for instance at a village where we were drawing buildings and had a chance to talk informally with local people. As well as an increased awareness of the built environment, the main gain was self expression. Shyness and inhibitions were gradually dispelled.' MARIANNE COXON

'I chose to work on *Art and the Built Environment* because it differed very much from the other subjects I was studying. It was very different to what I had expected. The group had ideas of their own and were allowed to voice them — it was not all teachers shouting out the orders and everyone obeying without uttering a word. I think one big problem however was that the study area was too large. It would have been better to concentrate on a small road.' RICHARD HEIN

It was found that the general studies course complemented not only studies undertaken by the A-level Art groups, but that of the CEE Environmental Studies. The following study brief is taken from an urban study (of Romsey, Hampshire), from that particular course.

Peter Symonds College: CEE Environmental Studies Course

1 **a** Find the following buildings or locations and mark them on the map provided:
Strongs' Brewery Old Town Hall
King John's House Corn Exchange
Duke's Mill
   b Apart from the brewery, explain what they are used for now.

2 Romsey contains a large number of old buildings, many of which were built in the Middle Ages. In common with other towns of similar size, many new buildings have also been added. In each case the architect has to decide whether to design a building which blends with the buildings which are already there, or a building which contrasts with them.
Select *one* new building which seems to fit in its surroundings, and *one* which does not. Mark both of them on the map provided. Explain why one appears to fit while the other does not.

3 Some areas near the centre of Romsey are not built on and are left empty or used for car parking. 2 such areas are marked with a number on the map. It could be argued that both sites could be put to a more suitable and more attractive use. Suggest a more appropriate use for *one* of these sites, using explanations and diagrams where necessary.

4 Traffic causes a number of problems in Romsey. Some problems are associated with through traffic using narrow streets; others with traffic bound for the centre trying to find a parking space.
   a *In Romsey:* find as many locations as you can where traffic (moving or stationary) causes a problem. Mark them on the map and state what the problem is.
   b *Homework:* suggest possible ways in which these problems might be solved.

Hartcliffe School

The study based at Hartcliffe Comprehensive School, Bristol consisted of a short course of 6 half-day sessions designed to promote a deeper perception of the built environment. This was set up by the Humanities Adviser of the Avon Education Department in response to an initiative from the local branch of the Royal Institute of British Architects which was anxious to make a contribution to environmental education. Although not strictly an *Art and the Built Environment* course, it had similar aims to those of the Project, concerned with developing environmental perception and enhancing discriminatory and critical skills. Students came from general studies courses at Hartcliffe School and from Merrywood Girls' School.

Members of the County architecture and planning departments contributed to this study in cooperation with a mixed team of teachers. The course was an experiment to determine the desirable content of a short environmental studies course suitable for sixth form general studies programmes, and to consider possible roles for members of the environmental professions in an educational context.

Planning sessions considered the possible scope and content of the study; possible learning and teaching methods; the need for a particular vocabulary or language to deal with the ideas and experiences involved, and understanding of the design processes and political processes which determine the form of the built environment. Practical considerations were also discussed: time, organization, study areas, resources, and the contributions which can be made by architects, planners and teachers. The following course outline was agreed, and it was decided to embark on the study in the second half of the spring term.

1 *Introduction*	exhibition; slide presentation; sensory exploration
2 *Townscape appraisal*	investigation of selected streetscapes
3 *Building appraisal*	investigation of selected buildings
4 *Other people's perceptions*	interviews with architects/users/residents
5 *Design problems*	game, simulation
6 *Presentations*	students' presentations of studies.

Worksheets were designed as aids to encourage a deeper response and to direct the learning activities. Sensory walk score, townscape assessment, building assessment (exterior), building assessment (interior) questionnaires were developed by individual groups to structure their interviews. The weather and other circumstances modified the course, and, as implemented, it took the following pattern:

Session 1: Introduction to a study of the built environment

The course was introduced by a slide presentation of townscape, and ideas for study. This was followed by a sensory walk in the local area in which students were divided into groups of 7 and dropped off at various points to avoid a very large group congregating together. Although the students seemed to grasp the nature of the study, they found the sensory walk difficult. This was perhaps because, although it demanded an enlarged subjective and emotional response, individuals were obliged to work within a group. This inhibited many students, even though they were dependent on the group for security. Much more time was needed for discussion so that students could assimilate ideas gained from the activity and so that teachers could gauge the level of response.

Session 2: Design problems

Because of bad weather, a townscape exploration and appraisal was not possible, so a school-based activity was substituted. The introduction that was used was a presentation of slides to illustrate the fact that we each inhabit our own perceptual world, and that there is no single correct description or interpretation of a selected environment, giving examples of possible differences, based on age, sex, social class, experience and interest.

This was followed by an exercise in the design of housing layouts, which was used to explore the way in which designers make compromises or 'trade-offs' between various design goals in order to reach an optimum solution. 12 small model houses, cut from strips of paper, as shown in the illustration, are to be arranged on an A4 plot, and various criteria are introduced to effect the design. There must be room for vehicle access, parking, pedestrian paths, play space, etc. Solutions may be rated, fairly or not, on the criteria of economy, expense, convenience, efficient land use, convenience for the user, and so on. Groups are asked to assess other groups' solutions, giving reasons for their opinions.

This kind of exercise encourages students to understand some of the problems and needs to be satisfied in urban design, and demonstrates, very simply, the types of compromise involved (see pages 76-77).

Session 3: Building study

Arrangements had been made for students to visit a number of modern or rehabilitated buildings — a church, a school, a factory, an old peoples' residence, an office and an arts centre. They were asked to make an appraisal of the building, assessing its qualities and giving reasons for their evaluation. The study briefs were useful here, particularly the one dealing with interiors, since because of the weather students did not have much opportunity to study the exteriors in their townscape context.

In some cases the architects responsible for the design met the students and showed them around the building, explaining the requirements or constraints which lay behind the design. To be shown round a building, however humble, by its designer is a privilege like discussing a book with its author, a painting with the artist or a piece of music with its composer. Since it depends on the architect being accessible and able to give up his time, it has to be seized upon whenever the chance occurs, but it is difficult to say what is the appropriate stage at which to introduce it. Those students who had an opportunity to explore the building on their own had a chance to respond directly and to form their own opinion of the place without being affected too soon by an 'official' perception. However, if the architect introduced his views later, the encounter might very well modify their view considerably, but at least the students would have had an opportunity to formulate their own opinion, rather than merely accept that of the expert.

Session 4: Further building study

On the second visit students were encouraged to discuss the buildings with the people who used them as residents or workers, and to compare their perceptions of them with their own and those of the architects. Questionnaires were prepared from discussions at the previous lesson, and helped to provide a basis for discussion. All the groups added to the basic list of questions and gained a great deal from talking to other people. Some interviews formed the basis of the presentations in later lessons, as they clearly demonstrated the different perceptions held by a number of people of the same building.

Session 5: Architect's role in the design process and role playing exercise

People are not usually clear about the role played by the architect, his client, the planning authority and the other branches of local government, in determining the ultimate form of the built environment. It was useful to consider how decisions are arrived at and what criteria might be used for reaching an evaluative judgement.

After a slide presentation on the work of the architect, which included plans, drawings, designs, sketches, work in progress and finished buildings, the groups were required to list their criteria for judging the suitability of a new office block. Each group was asked to assume a particular identity — that of planners, developers, clients, conservationists, and a subsequent comparison was made of their differing viewpoints.

Session 6: Presentations

In the final session students were asked to explain their experience of the course: what they had done, seen, found out, thought and felt, and why. All the presentations were concerned with the visits to actual buildings and the students managed to offer a reasonable account of these. All groups used slide programmes and some enacted interviews, putting forward the perceptions of the different people involved. At the end everyone was asked to evaluate the course and their own performance in it, using the following pointers for assessment:
- What was the aim of the course?
- How well was it organized?
- What help did you receive?

- What was the value of the worksheets?
- How might the course be improved?
- What have you learned from the study?
- What have you contributed to the study?
- Did you enjoy it?
- What sort of effort have you made?
- What kind of work have you done?
- How would you tackle a similar study differently?

A report was then prepared for members of the course team. Needless to say, they all had different perceptions of the study, each valuing different aspects and interpreting the outcomes differently. However, general conclusions were that the study was an example of the kind of co-operation needed between educational and environmental professionals. Undoubtedly this course highlighted the need to view environmental education in the context of the actual *shaping* of the environment. It also demonstrated how difficult it is to do this in a 6 session course, with students from a variety of backgrounds in environmental experience and understanding. (Indeed for some of them it had been their first experience of environmental study based on experiential learning.)

It is clear that although the general aims of the course were understood, all the specific objectives were not achieved. Teachers appreciated the detailed planning of each individual lesson, though others felt that the structure was too rigid and inflexible. However, students' comments indicated that they found it easier to work in situations which were clearly defined, where there was little doubt about ways of working, and where there were guidelines on which to act. This might be seen as over-directive, but it should be remembered that the situation of 2 schools working together on an environmental study was unfamiliar in itself, and that students needed security and support. It is not generally understood that the capacities for undertaking this kind of work are by no means natural attributes: they have to be learned.

Because of the excellent contribution by architects both to the planning and implementation of the course, teachers tended to take a rather passive stance. The adoption of teaching roles by architects and planners is not the most effective use that can be made of their particular wisdom. While teachers should be aware of the particular skills and expertise they have to offer, they should remember that the environmental professionals' concern is primarily with the environment; students' *educational* needs should be uppermost in teachers' minds.

There was some disagreement about the value of the worksheets. A number of architects and planners felt they had little value; the teachers thought they were helpful in directing learning activities; the students felt they were of great help in assisting them in identifying the problems that they faced.

Course evaluation

Recommendations were put in the form of a number of questions to be considered in the planning of future courses of this kind, and may very well be useful for art teachers involved in this kind of work:

Is everyone clear about the purpose and scope of the study?

What expertise and skill can the architects and planners contribute that is not available to the teachers already?

How do the architects' and planners' contributions differ from one another? How do they complement one another?

What is the possible interaction between teachers, architects and planners?

What intervention by the teacher is necessary? What means should be used to organize, direct and interpret learning activities?

What learning tasks are appropriate?

What ways of recording ideas and information are necessary?

What provision is there for both individual and group work?

How are experiential, thinking and communicatory capacities promoted?

How are discriminatory and critical skills developed?

What opportunities are there to discuss, interpret, assimilate experience?

How does it relate to students' previous studies?

How does it relate to other approaches to environmental studies?

How might the work be assessed? What evidence is there that the course has enhanced, extended, deepened students' experience, knowledge, perception of the built environment?

15 The 11-16 age range

The brief for our Project was specifically concerned with that minority of adolescents who remain within the care of the education system after the age of 16, but it is obvious that this work has relevance and importance for a much wider age range.

For this reason we include examples of work and of working methods from the experience of the younger age groups, both in trial schools in our Project and from other schools which have kindly made their experience available to us. The *Front Door* Project at Pimlico School, London, has been more fully documented than most and is the only example we have of a long-term art-based environmental study spanning the 7 years of secondary schooling. The table on the following page suggests a possible rationale for an all-through-the-secondary-school approach.

The experience of Ysgol Gyfun

Ysgol Gyfun, Istalyfera, is a Welsh-speaking comprehensive secondary school in one of the valleys of West Glamorgan. The head of the art department there, John James, believes that pupils have to achieve a certain level of receptivity to the aesthetic aspects of the environment before any useful degree of critical appraisal is possible. Consequently, in the earlier years of secondary education, he concentrates on providing a range of different kinds of sensory experience based upon environmental exploration. He is concerned with building up an adequate vocabulary, both visual and verbal, to cope with the demands of critical study.

A comparison was made between 2 classes in the same year group to determine the value of this kind of work with younger children. One class was given no experience of art-based environmental work and the other had an enriched course, lasting for most of the third year, when the greater part of their art work was based upon environmental exploration and the work resulting from it. Not only did this group produce very sensitive and interesting work showing a variety of subjects and study methods, but the pupils, when they entered the age-range with which our project is concerned, demonstrated a marked capacity for discrimination and criticism greater than that of their peers in the control group. John James remarks that 'it is at a later stage in their school lives that we expect to reap the rewards and benefits of this early activity'.

The development of the work in the lower school at Ysgol Gyfun evolved because of the obvious interest in this kind of work generated by the pupils, and partly because the Project work was not considered as specific and finite, but as a contribution to the development of an expanding department, willing to respond to the needs of pupils and keen to make use of stimuli and resources outside the school. A sensitive response to both people and place is a marked feature of this art department, and reflects its concern for the pupils, their ideas and their personal development.

When the pupils first come to the school, although it is not large when compared with many other secondary schools, they seem rather overwhelmed by the size and unfamiliarity of the organization of a comprehensive school, as many of them have come from very small village schools. An art lesson, once a week, separate from and unrelated to any other lesson, is particularly strange. John James recognizes that attitudes and habits established at this point will affect the rest of the pupil's involvement in art education. The working methods they encounter initially may be unknown, and the desire to do the right

People make judgements all the time within the limits of their personal exper‑ience and ability. However, this is not a fixed capacity but is liable to modifica‑tion, and merits direct intervention by the teacher to extend and develop his pupils' perceptual capabilities. The Project has not fully considered the developmental aspect, but proposes the following outline as a way of planning a long term course of studies. This should complement other approaches to environmental study. "The courses we teach are based on our own set of values as to what is imp‑ortant and significant in the environment. Perhaps it would be more constructive and creative if we were to try and base such courses on the value system of those we are teaching. That is to build on the percept‑ions and meanings that the child invests in his own environment." **David Uzzell.**	as a unit within courses such as: art: design: environ‑mental studies: liberal studies: community education				
		new to school environmental experience unknown	4 lessons	school and environs	enriched experience observing, record‑ing information
		increasing skills and confidence	6 lessons	neighbourhood	development of study skills based on visual/tactile modes
		stronger personal preferences and prejudices emerging	6 lessons	unfamiliar environment	development of discriminatory and critical skills
		growing social awareness	summer term	local area	relationship of aesthetic consider‑ations to social, historic, economic
		examination considerations	field trip after exams	contrasting area	development of expressive and communicatory skills
		personal research	as appropriate	personal choice	development of evaluative and critical skills

thing and satisfy the teacher's demands in a comparatively rigid and structured situation, so different from the cosy anarchy of the primary school, sometimes leads to a certain conformity and acceptance of other people's ideas. Mr James is well aware that many of the impressions of art and of art education are fixed in these first lessons and will affect the pupils' thinking and performance long afterwards.

To facilitate the entry into secondary education and to establish certain attitudes at the beginning, one of the early first year projects is based on sensory exploration of the school campus, and on work centred around the comparison of man-made and natural form. The department's particular interest here is to establish high levels of interest, motivation and standards of work.

In the second year, a different study environment is sought. This has included the seashore, acting as stimulus for all kinds of work — painting, drawing, cartoons, creative writing and tape-slide sequences. Although the children are Welsh-speaking and all the lessons are in Welsh, the standard of English is remarkably high: the school regularly competes in, and wins, English debating competitions.

Something of the flavour of the work in the second year can be gauged from this extract from a poem by a 12 year-old, Peter Hall:

. . . the sand has changed
ten hundred times its face
the wind wrinkles reflections
in the sea like lace
across the new born ridges
the spider crabs race
the rock does not go at any pace
it never changes its tear stained face.
. . .

The great number of funerals on the beach
great mounds two feet deep
wherein lie fathers fast asleep
they do not remember the war was here
it brought a new age of high rise fear
and the children play so near
to unremembered moments in the sand . . .

Drawings from younger pupils' village studies.

In the third year, with perhaps a sharpened perception and an eye ready to seek visual interest, a study is made of the village or some nearby locality. It is probably more difficult to encounter afresh the familiar place we take for granted than it is to confront the unknown, strange or unusual. But the first year's discovery of exotic fungi, or the second year's revelations in rock pools, can be matched by the fascination of derelict buildings, the robot-like appearance of ancient petrol pumps or the allure of faded names, of moss-covered grave-stones.

All these activities are, of course, under the supervision of the art teacher. But at the fourth and fifth year level it seemed appropriate to expect the pupils to work individually or to organize their own working groups in developing their own personal projects based on an exploration of a chosen environment. A variety of media are used: as well as painting and drawing, there are opportunities for work in ceramics, printing, textiles and photography. At sixth form level it has been found perfectly acceptable to incorporate the work in the A-level examination. The Welsh Joint Education Committee requires examples of course work, and there have been no problems for the students in providing it.

After nearly 3 years' involvement with the Project, John James's view of it is that 'the work is successful in enlarging pupils' awareness of the built environment, and as a consequence, helps them realize its potential as a source of creative stimuli.' Through its emphasis on the development of discriminatory and critical skills it has helped pupils to 'make judgements, and form opinions

about the built environment, and to appreciate and understand some of the environmental problems facing our society.'

He also makes a plea for the development of a critical vocabulary and for the provision of opportunities for pupils to analyse and discuss their experience, as well as to develop art work based on environmental reference.

'Art teachers will obviously show a strong bias in favour of visual feedback, possessing plenty of creative imagination. The results may be gratifying to the teachers as well as to those responsible for the work, but what has happened to the pupils during the process of producing these results? Their experience should not only lead to ''works of art'', it should also provide them with a method of communicating their ideas and attitudes developed through this experience, and this cannot be achieved by merely asking them to collect and record information. They should also have opportunities to discuss and analyse their experience as a basis for building a critical vocabulary.'

The school has found no problems in integrating the Project work with the rest of the art syllabus, and far from interfering with established art practices, the development of the pupil's capacity to respond to, understand and communicate their experience, has promoted, rather than hindered, the development of art skills. The Project also encourages a new relationship for the pupils with their environment:

'The Project made me look more closely at certain aspects of the built environment I usually took for granted.'

'I hardly ever go to this part of Ystalyfera, but since I have been involved in this Project, it has made me realize how certain environmental problems can affect the lives and attitudes of people who live here, and as a consequence, how these attitudes and the people involved can visually influence the environment.'

'Now that I have looked at the school from a different point of view, I realize more could be done to improve its general appearance.'

Coffin Row. A frame from a slide programme, 'Decay, Decline and Development', made by senior students.

Effective use of an unusual viewpoint.

Edgebarrow School's Wapping Project

At Edgebarrow School in Berkshire, fourth year art groups had been involved in environmental study as part of their art course, but teachers were not fully satisfied with the work, which they considered superficial and not up to the standard of other studies undertaken by the department. Staff felt that it was not enough just to examine arbitrarily an environment in the hope that pupils would respond creatively, but that they should be given some support in how to conduct and develop such a study.

To heighten pupils' response, it was thought that the study area should present an extreme contrast to their own local area, possibly an environment undergoing considerable change, with an easily accessible historical background, which highlighted the conflict of interests to which people might be subjected. Wapping was identified as a suitable study area, and the idea of metamorphoses considered as a focus for the study.

The art staff were also concerned to make a clear distinction as to how an art based approach to the environment might differ from other areas of the curriculum involved in environmental study, which were primarily concerned with the documentation of factual data. It was hoped that the shock of confronting a totally strange environment would have an emotional effect which would colour and personalize responses. However, because of the cost and the amount of organization necessary for such a venture, it was decided to use the day visit as a focus for a term's course, involving considerable preparation and follow-up work.

Preparation

Teachers met to discuss the possibilities for the study and to consider what preparation was necessary for the pupils in terms of heightening their expectations and sharpening their powers of observation. They also discussed strategies for investigation, ways of recording information and possible topics for study. Outside speakers were also invited to share their perceptions of the place, and it was hoped to encourage pupils to look at the environment in a more observant way, with greater sensitivity and a greater understanding of its effect on the lives of the people there.

Teachers visited the study area during the Christmas holidays and prepared suitable routes for small group study. Using their research, they briefed pupils on what to look for, how to observe, how to record information appropriately (e.g. sketch books, tape recorders, cameras, cine). Pupils were split into groups of 4, one teacher in charge of 5 groups. Each group chose to deal with a different topic (building fabric, colour, texture, people, shops, advertising, materials, street names, sounds, floorscape).

Appearance

A list of ideas was prepared for all the pupils to consider (see below). This list of categories is by no means complete — you may already have thought of others. Nor should you at this stage settle cosily for any one of them, thus closing your mind to other possibilities. This list is merely an aid to your observations to help you sort them out, and make you aware of the vast number of items where your interest might centre itself, and lead you into your work.

Organization of the course

The timetable for the course was as follows:
DECEMBER
Planning meetings to define study, to articulate rationale and aims, to provide a general picture of intentions. Teachers to visit study area to decide on routes, possible topics for study.

Some ideas as aids to observation:

Materials *their metamorphosis or transformation through:*

wood	
clay	decay
stone	erosion
iron	impact
steel	fragmentation (through decay, erosion or impact)
glass	accretion (through spillage or spread)
water	distortion (through pressure, twisting, bending)
paint	oxidization (exposure)
enamel	vegetation (overgrown, destroyed)
fabric	also, change in functional status — e.g. shops boarded up or used as something else
plastic	

Objects

skylines	waterfronts	windows	names
chimneys	factories	doorways	lettering
towers	railways	lamp posts	advertising signs
structures	dwellings	street signs	rubbish areas
facades	pubs	bollards	drain covers
frontages	boats	pavements	machines (in use)
play areas	no-go areas	animals, birds	machines (obsolete)

Sounds

Smells

People *talking (accents) about:*
themselves
their work
their family
their environment
its history, present, future

JANUARY

1 Audio-visual show to introduce study area and ideas for study based on teachers' research

2 Briefing groups on general organization

3 Illustrated talk by Colin Ward, TCPA Education Officer

4 Briefing session, discussion, start of topic group formation

5 Head of resources — use of audio-visual equipment

6 Topic groups; topics briefing

7 Trial run in Crowthorne

8 Collation, re-allocation, discussion of topic groups

9 Allocation of equipment; preparation of visit

10 Visit to Wapping

11 Collation of data
8 further sessions for studio development of the work
2 sessions for exhibition preparation

Streetwork

The timetable for the day visit was:
9.30 – 12.30   streetwork — exploration, investigation, recording information
12.30 – 1.00   lunch
1.00 – 2.15   drawing

Each member of the small groups was assigned a particular role — photographer, interviewer etc. Some equipment was provided by the school, and some by the pupils themselves. The groups were set down at various points, given a map, allocated a study area and given instructions to arrive at the meeting point at 1.00.

Development

The initial lessons after the streetwork were taken up with discussion about the investigations, and the possible directions further development of the work might take. 8 further sessions were allocated to develop artwork based on the streetwork, and pupils allocated to a particular media area and teacher in accordance with the department's usual rotation system. Pupils were told that the work would be exhibited, and that it should show clearly what their personal response to the place had been. This gave the pupils a specific goal, and a particular pressure of time. The work might also be included in their examination course work, so motivation and commitment was high.

Comments

Teachers felt that the preparatory period had perhaps been too long, resulting in some loss of spontaneity, but the quality of the work was high, and the pupils seemed to develop a wider understanding of the subject matter than previously had been the case. Pupils of low ability sustained a high involvement in the work — all members of the group managed to pitch the project at their own level of interest and ability. All members of the group developed different perceptions of Wapping, and it helped a number of them see their familiar environment of Crowthorne afresh.

Students certainly were led to develop a greater understanding of the study area than is normally the case in art based environmental studies at this level, as they were given a lot of historical and sociological information as background for their own investigations, which perhaps provided a frame of reference. The danger in this of course is that teachers' perceptions may be projected onto pupils, rather than pupils being encouraged to develop their own. However, the Wapping study emphasized the need for direct experience and close observation and provided lots of opportunities for discusion and comparison of points of view.

Students' opinions

'I'm not sure if the teachers knew quite the extent to which the work would reach. The original idea seemed to escalate dramatically, and the exhibition at the end was of a very high standard, and even overshadowed some of the CSE work with it. Occasionally things happen in the course of my life which make me very aware of how lucky I am to live where I do, and the trip to Wapping, quite a sordid area, made me realize this. It wasn't an area which was unliveable in, it was just the atmosphere — very hostile, especially towards children — and the way everything looked. Most things were dirty, thick with grime, though I was surprised at the lack of litter. There were lots of signs restricting anyone from doing anything, and this added to the hostility. It seemed the sort of place where you could live for years and years and not know your next door neighbour's name. Crowthorne is clean. Wapping is not. Crowthorne has a free feeling about it. Wapping has not. I think it helped a lot of people to think in perspective about their way of life compared to other people's. I think the project could have stretched over to other subjects — English perhaps.' HELEN KNIGHT

'We spent about 5 weeks planning our project — I thought this was a bit long. We knew what we were going to look for when we got there (our group did chimneys and skylines). We were told so much about it that there was little left to our imagination. Of course we needed some time to plan the project beforehand, but perhaps 2 weeks would have been enough. In a way, Wapping looked as I thought it would, but still different as I hadn't actually seen it before. When I got back I already knew how I would do my piece of work. I did pottery, and in our group we didn't find much use for the photographs we had taken. The sketches we made were more useful — also what we remembered but had not put down as drawing or writing. However, some other people needed photographs to work from. All in all, the Project was very worthwhile. The Wapping exhibition was good and it was interesting to see how every member of the fourth year could have a different view of the same place. I thought it was a good idea to choose a place so different from

Crowthorne, and we had practice in looking at a place as artists, and not just glancing at it as so many people would.'   ANNA BENGTSSON

'My first impression of Rotherhithe was that it seemed a horrible place and I would not like to live there. Many of the buildings were old, some had windows smashed or boarded up, others were just in need of repair. Nearly all the rest were three or four storeyed flats and also there were a couple of shops. None of the houses I saw had gardens and there was only one large park for children to play. It wasn't until we actually spoke to people who lived in Rotherhithe that we realized what the place was really like to live in. Nearly all the people liked living there. They found the other people friendly. Some said they would never move away from the area. Rotherhithe *needed* to be a friendly place. If it wasn't it would be a horrible place to live in. The area around Crowthorne where I live, looks nice, nearly all the houses have gardens, but in some places the people don't even know the name of their next door neighbour. Wapping, on the other side of the river, was very different. There were many roads with empty warehouses, making them very dark. The condition of the houses people live in are very terrible. I think I would rather live in the area I am living in now, for on the whole I feel it is a much better place to live in.'   DERRY EVANS

'We should have gone on the trip about one or two weeks after the beginning of term. That way we would have had more time and more interesting things to do at the beginning of the new term. However, we did obtain some valid points before the trip, but I thought too much time was spent on silly little details, such as trying to find art in squashed cans. All right, you can find art in the strangest places, but I think that in some areas of the project this was overdone. Some people may have thought the whole project a bit of a bore, but as for me, from a personal opinion, I thought the term was well used. It gave me an insight into new ways of presenting work, and kept me occupied with a good selection of interesting things to do. I think the best benefit for me came from the prints I did.'   NIGEL RATCLIFFE

Conclusions

The Edgebarrow School Project demonstrates the conflict between spontaneity and structure: the need to heighten pupil's capacity for response, without overloading. This particular project had its origin in the art teachers' desire to confront the fourth-year students with the experience of Wapping, by putting them all in a furniture van and dumping them in the study area. This initial idea was soon modified, not least by the fact that it cost £80 to transport the students to Wapping. From some points of view the subsequent elaboration of the exercise took away from its experiential value. All projects of this kind are faced with this particular tension, and the teachers' decision as to how much time is to be allotted to preparation, streetwork and follow-up has to be a matter of professional judgement — or guesswork and intuition — based on the teachers' knowledge of the pupils involved.

Sheredes School

Sheredes School at Hoddesdon was particularly interesting as a trial school as it was one of the two associated with the Project which adopt a 'common core' policy, where all pupils follow a similar course of studies before choosing options for sixth form study. In the aspect of the curriculum with which we are concerned, this meant that all students followed an art and design course for 5 years, and took the CSE examination at the end of this period.

Maurice Holt, the first headmaster of the school, explains in his book *The Common Curriculum* (Routledge, 1978) that

'it makes sense for a creative activities faculty to concentrate in the first two or three years of a five year course, on an approach which uses, like humanities, a weak theory of integration and develops skills through mainly instructional objectives; moving in the fourth and fifth years to a problem-centred approach developing skill through stronger integration and expressive objects.'

In the first 3 years a rotation system is developed with pupils experiencing a variety of materials and working methods.

'In the fourth and fifth years, there is a distinct shift. Staff are allocated to three groupings: human aids and extensions; living and working space; and communications. These are concerned respectively with ergonomics and craft skills; problems of direct experience (new designs, model making) and problems related to forms of expression in visual communication using signs and symbols (art work; a critical approach to advertising). 45% of the marks in the concluding CSE Mode Three examination go to the pupils' fourth year course work, as a recorded design process and as a final product, 55% for the final project and diary in the fifth year. In this way each student is led to find autonomy in making his own aesthetic judgements, based on a broad general education in subject structures which reflect art as a form of life.

Criticisms of such design courses have been that there is a lack of continuity and depth of study because of the rotation system, that close working relationships between teachers and pupils are difficult to develop, and that too much emphasis is placed on what has been called a 'materials circus.' Art teachers also complain that the time actually given to art is drastically cut, and the result is a certain superficiality of approach.

Our experience with the students at Sheredes suggests that the Creative Activities Faculty there has managed to avoid the pitfalls through sensitive management, and has capitalized on the strengths of such a scheme to develop a long-term course of studies based on visual/tactile modes which is seen as a necessary and basic part of everyone's educational experience.

In terms of our own Project, this certainly seemed to be an advantage, for all the first-year sixth form students in the Central Studies course possessed a remarkable degree of confidence and familiarity with visual/tactile modes and responded more easily and readily to the demands of this

particular kind of study, than students in other schools without this enriched background in art education. This was particularly evident in their response to the notion of the sensory walk, which was less inhibited than that we found in many other schools, while the experience itself was more fully exploited. These students' ability to consider choices of media in relation to the ideas they wished to communicate was particularly sensitive, and reflected their previous experience in visual communication.

We were particularly interested in some of the projects that involved pupils before the sixth form study in which we were involved. These included, in the second year, maps of routes in Hertfordshire, in the third year, landscape studies and 3-dimensional work on stage design, and in the fifth year, models exploring spatial qualities, a study of Hoddesdon, and ceramic models evoked by the photographs in Ivor de Wolfe's *The Italian Townscape* (Architectural Press, 1963).

We concluded that this background of experience and exploration was the explanation of the remarkable work by sixth form students in our own project, and that it would have been equally valuable in a sixth form course with other objectives.

Kingsthorpe Upper School

Kingsthorpe School in Northampton is a senior comprehensive school (for the 13–18 age range) whose education policy is also based on the idea of a core curriculum. All pupils follow a 3 year course of study in the creative arts faculty, and take one or more art, craft or design examinations at the end of the fifth year.

Our interest was particularly in the third and fourth year courses, where a variety of environments were used as a basis for study. These included a canal, allotments, the high road, housing developments and the school campus itself. The time in each year is split between 'basic' and 'resource' courses. A particular teacher is responsible for each class and develops a basic course concerned with the development of a visual language of line, colour, texture, tone, etc. Classes also have the opportunity to work in other areas with different specialists during the resource courses, which are primarily media based.

'The main aim of each resources programme should be to give the students a grounding and knowledge in the appropriate techniques and tools, materials and language involved in each area to facilitate the work from the basic course.'

A strong emphasis is placed on the interrelationship of ideas and experience between the two types of course. Teachers are expected to know of the work in other areas and pupils are encouraged to familiarize themselves with all the work that goes on in the faculty.

'Teachers should plan carefully and share awareness of each others' programmes. It is important that everyone is *au fait* with what is being taught in each material area, and each teacher should demonstrate to colleagues what he is doing, and students should perhaps make occasional well-planned excursions into the other areas to share demonstrations and to see the work of the other students in their group.'

Work based on environmental reference has been well established in this department for a long time. The staff are concerned with the development of a visual vocabulary and its relevance and importance in our daily lives. They describe the aims of the third year course as learning to see, to discriminate, evaluate, communicate and to present evidence of this by graphic means.

'Front Door' at Pimlico

The *Front Door* Project was originally conceived by Ken Baynes in a paper given at the Institute of Contemporary Arts in London on 5 October 1973 (published in the *Bulletin of Environmental Education* in February 1974). He proposed an architectural education programme which would involve architects from the Greater London Council Department of Architecture and Civic Design in direct contact with teachers and children. The Inner London Education Authority's Art Inspectorate steered this initiative towards Pimlico School, a large, inner-city comprehensive school with 1760 pupils, and the experiment took shape there during the years 1974–1976, aiming at devising a sequential pattern of art-based investigation of the urban environment.

The first year pupils studied the concept of neighbourhood. This involved local trails, streetwork, museum visits and follow-up work in the classroom. Everything was related to the local environment or to the children's own neighbourhood, and information and ideas were expressed through drawing, painting and writing.

Typical studies in this scheme were an investigation of the journey to school, a Pimlico trail, necessitating a museum visit to check up on the background to the development of the area, a study of the individual child's own home and its surroundings (the school has a very wide catchment area) and an exploration of the relationship of the child to each, his views about them

1st year streetscape

and ideas for improvement, with a glimpse of future possibilities.

The second year work concentrated purely on the exploration and development of visual ideas: line, shape, pattern, texture and colour. This work demanded close observation, careful visual analysis and the development of ideas in a variety of media. Drawing was a means of focussing attention, holding concentration and analysing information.

Because of complexities of school organization it was not possible to operate a third year study as a natural development from the first two years, but in the proposed scheme, the third year course would be based on the consideration of the environment as a changing reality and the various human activities which affect it and have to be accommodated in proposals about the way in which this adaptation could be improved. Basic human activities which could be investigated are playing, learning, growing up, growing old, communication, buying and selling, and moving about.

The work in the fourth year for pupils in the community education programme continued the visual bias, but was closely related to the social environment. The choice of subjects could equally well have been made by a social studies group: housing, play provision, transport, 'words in town', shops, but the method of study and the presentation of ideas was different, stressing the importance of visual material in communicating ideas. The most satisfactory way of working seemed, for a number of reasons, to be through the making of slide programmes. The pupils worked in pairs, chose their own subject for study, and were asked to make a programme of 30 slides with a taped commentary, suitable for showing to other fourth

2nd year church

3rd year shopfront

4th year   Battersea Power Station

5th year   Fulham gasworks

6th year   riverfront

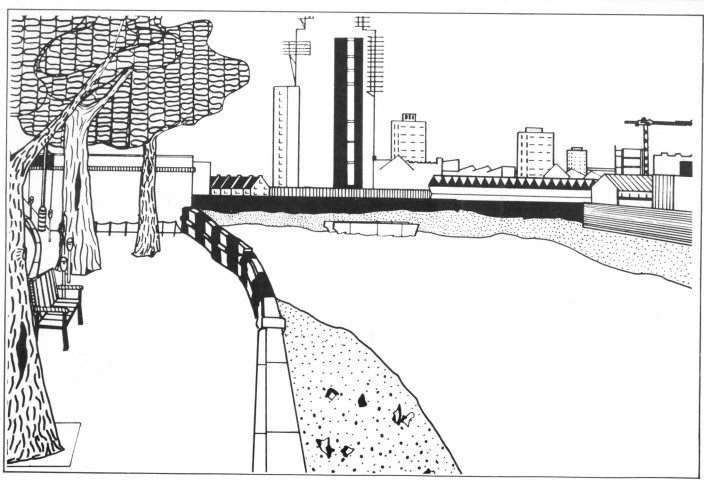

year groups in social studies, or as stimulus material for the lower school groups. This approach was welcomed by the pupils, who rapidly became very proficient in photography.

Through this activity the team and pupils were involved in making two filmstrips with the Schools Broadcasting Council. The first was the BBC Radiovision slide/tape presentation 'Shopping in Town' in the Art and Humanities series on *Everyday Architecture* devised by Colin Ward. This programme looked at the 'signals' transmitted to potential customers by the display of goods and design in shops, and contrasted the scale of traditional shops and shopping with supermarkets. In it pupils were told about the visual basis of retail display, not by the art teacher but by the local delicatessen proprietor and the ironmonger.

The second of these slide/tape programmes was for the Study Box, 'Front Door — Broadcasting and the Architectural Environment' which is about the Project as a whole and shows the fourth year students working on their slide programmes. This is available on loan for teacher education from the Schools Broadcasting Council.

The medium of study was also that of communication: using a camera to record information, to make visual statements, to express opinions and ideas. The slides and photographs taken by the fourth

year students were used as resource material by other classes and were available to any department wanting to borrow them. The pupils could see their work being tested on second year classes as an introduction to visual study. This improved motivation and made demands on the pupils for certain standards of effort and quality, as they realized that their work had value for others as well as themselves.

Other fourth year pupils in some of the art groups were able to develop study of the local area through drawing and painting, with outdoor sketching sessions for work which was developed further in the art room. This type of study was well suited to the CSE and GCE O-level Art courses.

Out of 5 working terms spent in preparation for CSE and O level, 3 in the fourth year and 2 in the fifth, one term — the summer term of the fourth year — was used for art work based on environmental exploration (that is, 20 per cent of the time available). In the sixth year the work was cast in the form of a liberal studies option and encountered several of the problems with which we have since become familiar in the *Art and the Built Environment* Project.

One of the aims of the *Front Door* Project had been to assess the possible role of local authority architects in the improvement of the architectural education of the ordinary schoolchild. The lessons to be drawn from this involvement are described in Chapter 16.

shops

interview

open space

where we live

Part Four:
Conclusions

16 The Significance of the Project and its future development

The working experience

The various courses, schemes and projects documented in the previous sections provide evidence of the range and scope of *Art and the Built Environment* work, currently promoted in schools. Most courses are concerned with the first aim of the Project: to develop environmental perception, through raising levels of response, sensitivity and awareness. Because of the dominance of media based studies in art examination courses, the development of critical skills in relation to environmental appraisal has been most noticeable in general studies courses. Drawing on experience from Phase Two, however, we can now say with confidence that art teachers can use art as a medium for developing critical skills and that the examinations, even without change, can support them.

In Phase One, we found the art teacher to be the most important factor in determining the nature and scope of the work, the quality of the learning experience and the study methods used. In all studies, teachers have been concerned with problems of planning, organization and assessment.

Planning

In planning courses teachers should give some attention to the age and previous experience of the pupils involved and to the level of perceptual development that can be expected of them so that the study is relevant and can build on and extend their previous experience. It is also important to consider the particular skills and capacities the course is intended to promote. It is not particularly useful just cheerfully to tell children to respond to an environment without structuring the experience in some way to give it a deeper significance for them. Careful thought should be given to the preparation for the study which students receive. If this is to be concerned with developing their perception of the environment, teachers should not seek to impose their own views upon the study area, but should provide students with ways of understanding and appraising it.

As well as the physical environment itself, there are other resources which the teacher may draw upon, such as the people who live and work there, together with those in environmental professions like architects or planners. Phase Two is building on this connection and already provides a coherent framework for inter-professional cooperation.

We have found that their most successful contributions are in response to specific demands rather than to vague requests for help. Architects can offer valuable assistance in helping teachers identify possible study subjects as well as with ways of appraising the environment. They can also 'open up' the school to the community and provide an essential impetus for curriculum development.

Organization

How the study is introduced seems to be a key element in the success or failure of the work. Expectations should be made clear at the outset, and working methods identified. However, it is not advisable to introduce too much other information too soon, before students have had an opportunity to come to terms directly with the environment themselves.

It also seems evident that the success of particular studies is very much dependent on the quality of the streetwork sessions. This does not relate to the time spent in the environment, but to the quality of the experience and the depth of response. Of course, half day sessions are preferable for streetwork — the amount of time available for study will depend on the school timetable and the accessibility of the study area. It is advisable to have a briefing session at the beginning and a plenary session at the end of streetwork expeditions, so that everyone is clear what is expected, and reports back. Block timetabling is therefore very helpful, but not absolutely necessary. Resourceful teachers have used lessons before and after lunch to give a bit of breathing space, or set streetwork investigation as homework.

We have found that the most successful streetwork sessions have been those where students have had clear objectives, a study brief and specific methods identified for study. Pressure of time is not always a bad thing, as sometimes this encourages students to focus more readily and develop an intensity in their work that is not necessarily apparent in more relaxed conditions. If the study area is unfamiliar, students need to have clear maps and identified meeting places. The question of supervision is of course an important one. Schools promoting this kind of study tend to organize class work under the supervision of a teacher in the first 3 years, to encourage group study in the fourth and fifth year, leading to individual study for older students. If pupils are used to environmental work, and parents are informed that this will be included in the course and necessary safety precautions are taken in the selection of study areas, then we do not anticipate any particular difficulties. Some schools take it for granted that pupils of all ages may be occupied on unsupervised work outside the school; for others, the very idea is anathema, and the bugbear of insurance and potential hazards is always raised. Streetwork, with its direct experience is, however, *essential* to the study methods.

A study of *Art and the Built Environment* is not a solitary exercise. There needs to be opportunity for group interaction and general discussion of ideas and experiences. Attitudes perhaps unique to the individual are shaped by group response and social conditioning. This should be recognized and used positively by the teacher. It is often better to be alone during an exploration in order to concentrate on one's own thoughts and feelings and to record a personal response. But we have found that group interaction and support is necessary for the development of a critical vocabulary. As well as developing visual means of communication, students should be encouraged to explain and comment on their experience, to discuss and argue. There need to be opportunities for students to compare their own perceptions with those of others, to modify, augment and deepen their understanding through shared knowledge. This may be done through discussion with colleagues, and many of the assessment sheets suggested are merely ways of recording information as a basis for comparison. Or one may compare one's own perceptions of a place with those of residents or established authorities, such as critics, historians or architects.

The lesson immediately following the streetwork session also appears to be crucial in determining the further development of the work. Teachers should consider ways of helping students interpret and assimilate the experience of streetwork, and indicate how they might present a considered personal view which demonstrates evidence of discriminatory and critical skills in relation to an appraisal of the environment. It has been evident from the work of the trial schools that visual imagery alone does not communicate a critical response: the art teacher must find ways to help students arrive at satisfactory forms of communication in this context.

We found that the critical aspect of the work was not adequately covered by the traditional curriculum or by the media-dominated art course. We do not accept that the curriculum is already overcrowded or that art examination syllabuses do not permit critical study. We are not seeking to introduce yet another new subject into an already full timetable, but simply recognition of a neglected aspect of art education. We think art teachers should look critically at their present art courses and consider how they relate to all the pupils in the school. The examination syllabuses should be reconsidered in relation to this kind of work and alternative possibilities considered.

We have also found that the Project's ideas are more likely to be developed in schools where the work is easily integrated into existing art courses, or where general studies programmes are flexible enough to accommodate this type of study. It is therefore necessary for art teachers to know something of the curriculum planning policy in their school, and of possible alternatives in timetabling arrangements.

Assessment

Many teachers are concerned with the problems of assessing this type of work. They might consider what evidence is presented to show that students' environmental perception has been enlarged; whether there has been an increase in environmental sensitivity and awareness; whether there has been an improvement in discrimination and critical skills. These might be seen from observing learning processes, students' work and comments.

Robert Witkin is helpful here and advises

'The most obvious evidence (for assessment) will be in changes of attitude demonstrated by the student as he moves through different problems. Does he use a wide range of resources as a basis for problem solving? Does he continually consider alternatives or get stuck with one solution? Does he consider problems both in visual and tactile terms? Does he translate from one form to another? Does he value uniqueness and integrity? Does he give evidence of being visually aware and discriminating? Is his perception of the world sharper?'

Teachers might also ask themselves the following questions: How was the students' environmental experience enriched? How was their understanding of the environment enlarged, deepened? What development has there been in vocabulary — both visual and verbal? What working relationships have been established or exploited? What new directions for thinking have been suggested? Which study methods have succeeded, which have failed? Why?

It is necessary for teachers to consider their own contribution to the learning activity, and they should seek not only to assess the work of individual students, but to consider the development of the course as a whole. In curriculum development, teachers need to be self-critical, and to be able to analyse their own work so that changes might be made for future courses. This kind of evaluation is being promoted in Phase Two and techniques are being developed to help make it a normal part of the work.

Aspects of the study that teachers might consider are the kind of preparation that was necessary, the arrangements that had to be made, the organization of the study, timetable modifications, the involvement of other teachers or people outside the school. They should consider the experience of the streetwork; the study methods used in the research and in the classroom follow-up; the type of support and direction provided by the teacher; the provision made for explanation, discussion, argument; the type of work undertaken, its relevance, degree of complexity, time taken for the study.

Examinations

During the course of the Project we have worked with students in both examination and non-examination groups. In the 16–19 age range we have contributed to both A-level Art and A-level Design courses. These syllabuses in the case of most of the examination boards provide adequate opportunity for environmental work, though perhaps they underplay the critical aspect and fail to make it sufficiently explicit. However, we have met no examiners who would not welcome developments which promote higher levels of personal insight and critical thinking.

We are convinced that the problem is not so much the wording of the syllabuses as the teachers' interpretation of them. It is inevitable in any subject that we are tempted to assume that what has been successful one year will always be successful, and that if we have found a winning formula we should stick to it. This of course is contrary to the spirit of the examinations themselves, above all in subjects like art and design.

When the Project was initiated it was suggested that we should prepare a draft syllabus based on this kind of work and submit it to one of the boards for consideration as a 2-year A-level course. But in practice we felt obliged to reject this idea because we do not see this work as a specialist study for an interested minority of students, for our whole case is that it is relevant and important for everyone.

We therefore prefer to see the work as a unit in a larger art course, or as part of a general studies course or of an environmental studies programme. We do not propose it as an alternative to established art courses, nor as a specialist option for the tiny minority who may be future architects or planners or designers.

Certain examination boards go a long way to satisfying the Project's need for adequate emphasis on course work and the development of critical skills. A review of syllabuses was carried out. This showed decisively that the existing syllabuses could be used.

The importance of the art teacher

'There can be no significant innovation in education that does not have at its centre the attitudes of teachers, and it is an illusion to think otherwise. The beliefs, assumptions, feelings of teachers are the air of the learning environment: they determine the quality of life within it.'

NEIL POSTMAN and CHARLES WEINGARTNER
Teaching as a Subversive Activity

At first we were confused by the many apparent teaching styles and educational philosophies demonstrated by the art teachers with whom we came in contact. We have been helped to understand certain patterns by commentators like Maurice Barrett, who defines 6 basic rationales adopted by art teachers at present: the arts and crafts approach; the fine arts approach; conceptual art; visual education; graphicacy and design education.[1]

The last of these reflects the pressures on art departments in the past decade to become part of larger inter-disciplinary units which are intended to coordinate art, technical studies and home economics. Another such grouping involves art, music and drama, linked by a common concern with expression and performance. Yet another recent form of amalgamation is media studies — perhaps art, English and social studies, linked by sociological preoccupations. The situation has become further complicated by the confused and defensive stance of some art teachers who feel threatened not only by what they see as take-over bids from other departments, but by the many and complex demands made on them.

Curriculum development projects like our own do not operate on neutral ground in an open situation. All the teachers with whom we have been working have brought to the Project their accumulated experience, interests, enthusiasms, biases and prejudices, and represent a wide range of attitudes in relation to education, to art and to the built environment.

The most important factor in determining the quality of the learning experience for the students is the attitude that the teacher brings to the job. The art teacher's self-concept, his interpretation of his role, appears to be one of the main factors determining how he operates and what he teaches.

Because of their training, art teachers are used to looking at the environment as artists. They produce powerful and original images which reflect their personal response to the stimulus of townscape. They observe carefully what other people take for granted, or establish relationships where none existed before, drawing on the environment for their own work. Many find difficulty in viewing it as critics.

Some art teachers assume, perhaps unconsciously, that a repetition of their own training is what is required in schools. Some are unwilling to consider the possibility that children in schools may have different educational requirements from those of art students in higher education.

Many heads of departments responsible for sixth form work involved in our Project, have trained as painters and promote work which is largely image-making and 2-dimensional. They may feel threatened when alternative modes of study are presented as appropriate for an art course in general education, as they feel it is outside their experience and control. They may see alternative approaches as questioning the image they have of themselves as teachers of art, and the value of the work they have done previously. Many teachers feel happier in the role of artists initiating others into the skill of their art or craft, than as teachers using art as a medium for the development of perception. Their emphasis is on art as expression, rather than as a vehicle for initiating, exploring and organizing experience, a means of perceiving, a framework for dealing with value judgements.

It is not a myth that many art teachers are art school graduates who have chosen teaching as a second choice occupation. They see themselves as artists rather than as teachers, and consider a watered-down version of their professional training in art as a suitable programme for art in general education. Malcolm Ross describes their attitude very well in his Schools Council Working Paper *Arts and the Adolescent*: 'with the sixth form I can really be myself, as an artist who teaches rather than as art teacher.'[2]

At first, the art teachers were resistant to the idea of critical study. They had a negative attitude towards the built, in contrast to the natural, environment and were sceptical about its shaping through architecture and planning. For them, it epitomized the harsh realities of life as against a romantic view of nature evident in much painting and sculpture. Many saw criticism as a negative activity except in relation to art history and could not make a similar connection with architecture. Where they attempted it, a number tended to project their own feelings and ideas about it, rather than base the study on the pupils' experience and perceptions. Their attitudes had in the first place been formed through their professional training as artists and their initial training as teachers. These were reinforced by the schools' expectations of what an art teacher is and should do. How they approached *Art and the Built Environment* work was affected by their perception of their role, the degree of personal interest and involvement in environmental concerns and personal qualities of confidence, security and self-assurance. These influenced their willingness and ability to experiment and innovate.

One of our most successful teams comprised a teacher whose background was that of a landscape painter, with another teacher whose background was in interior design. They both applied ideas from these areas to a study of townscape and exterior environments. But, in general, art teachers have been slow to take responsibility for environmental education, whether as a study in its own right or as part of an interdisciplinary approach. Perhaps they resent the possibility of art becoming merely a servicing agent for other subject disciplines whose contribution to environmental education has been much more clearly defined. Yet, the Project showed clearly that their contribution is vital.

The teacher, secure in the traditional role of expert in the classroom, is perhaps unwilling to see himself as learner, to focus on things to which he had previously paid scant attention, to enlarge and modify his own perception, though at the same time he expects precisely these things of his pupils. It is perhaps not the inflexibility either in departmental structures or the physical organization of the school that is the main difficulty in coping with work of this kind, but rather the inflexibility of some teachers' attitudes. Education is necessarily concerned with relationships and we should consider what attitudes, concepts and skills we wish to develop in our pupils, and use these as a basis for communicating with each other.

If these comments seem negative they need to be put in the perspective of the enthusiasm and commitment that the Project has aroused. Its success and its extension to a further decisive phase of development has depended on the ability and willingness of art teachers to take up the challenge posed by this concern with the environment and to relate their discipline to it. They need to accept and deal with their professional responsibilities as educators. This affects in particular their ability to see the curriculum as a dynamic reality requiring a capacity to view change positively and purposefully. Here the Project and fresh directions in art teaching have come together to the benefit of teachers and pupils. The result is a more realistic form of art and design education strongly related to the everyday experience of the pupils involved.

Current progressive thought in art education believes it necessary for art teachers to take a more positive stance. In the immediate past, pressures on the curriculum and the general isolation of art from the community has led to a defensive attitude and self-imposed limitations. Art teachers have felt safer within the confines of the studio and have not been effective in helping young people deal with contemporary culture. But this is an important and necessary aspect of their job. *Curriculum 11-16* says:[3]

> 'Tradition and precedent is less useful now as a guide in a situation of accelerating change, and therefore there is more need for an enhanced constructive sense of judgement. Whether we respond, for example to new consumer products, to fresh artistic manifestations or to change in the environment with concern, self-confidence and good judgement, or on the contrary with a vulnerable lack of awareness, depends in part on the quality of the educational process.'

Art teachers should be encouraged to take a much wider view of their role than they do at present, and should pay more attention to the needs of their pupils, rather than to the demands of their subject.

In asking art teachers to reconsider the extent of their role and to make provision for a richer experience for their pupils, the Project is attempting to establish a wider range for art in general education. *Art and the Built Environment* is just one of a number of possible contributions to this development.

If art teachers do not choose to concern themselves with critical appraisal of the built environment, the work will remain undone, for there are no other teachers in most schools who have the potential skills and knowledge to involve themselves in this difficult area that links aesthetics and subjectivity with critical awareness and involvement in the community. Many teachers may have to be convinced of the importance of the ideas and the value of their own particular contribution before they can begin to think about incorporating them into their teaching programmes and before they can concentrate on developing approaches to study and working methods. The Project offers teachers strong arguments and a firm working basis on which they can build.

Recent developments

Working parties

One of the key questions in curriculum development in recent years has been the problem of dissemination. It is one thing to identify good practice and see it put to use in the special conditions of a limited number of trial schools, quite another to see it have a wider influence on the education system as a whole. Many excellent approaches have foundered in this way, their influence limited to the small circle of those involved in the first experiments.

It happened that a number of experiences with the Project suggested a possible form of future development. Even before *Art and the Built Environment* began, *Front Door* (see pages 000-000) had shown that the design professions might have a role to play in curriculum development in this area. That idea was reinforced by the example of the Hampshire Association for Art Education and their contribution to the Project. In both cases the impetus for change came from a working contact between teachers, architects and planners. It was from these beginnings that the idea of *Art and the Built Environment* working parties developed. Clearly they are not the only way ahead but they do represent a particularly useful model which, with local variations, is already proving to be widely applicable.

In recent years, there have been numerous examples of architects and teachers cooperating in educational ventures, but generally these have been particular and limited — in competitions, award schemes and special projects, such as European Architectural Heritage Year.

Working parties differ in that members offer a long term commitment to work together to establish appropriate study techniques and courses in schools for pupils to develop a more critical understanding of their environment. The aim of this partnership is permanently to affect educational practice in order to prepare pupils to take a more creative and participatory stance in shaping their environment in adult life. The evidence is that this aim can be realized.

Members come together in meetings and individuals make further arrangements to work together — either to plan courses or to work directly with children. Seminars and courses are also organised to enable members to develop appropriate study methods and report on work already undertaken. Key figures are particular architects and planners who coordinate the involvement of their colleagues and local authority advisers who provide links with teachers and schools. It is evident that without their encouragement and support, architects and planners would have no real access to schools. Teachers commit themselves to experiment and to report on their studies, are responsible for documenting the work and disseminating it locally. Architects and planners can offer advice and support in terms of the scope and content of possible studies and ways of tackling them. However, it is soon evident that this advice is much more relevant and worthwhile when they have had direct experience of children in schools, so, where possible, they are invited to work directly with teachers and children to find out how children learn. Architects and planners are very well aware of the constraints on the designer. They also need to understand that the present school system imposes serious constraints on learning.

By May 1981, 50 such working parties were planned or in existence and it is now clear that architects and planners can introduce new kinds of expertise and knowledge, and offer alternative perceptions and interpretations that are valuable to teachers and their pupils.

Teachers are being asked to develop a critical stance to their own work, and colleagues are asked to share their experience so that others might learn from it. This is not an easy task, involving as it does a reconsideration and expansion of the teacher's role, while attempting to cope with the demands and exasperations of a busy school life. But it is precisely this kind of 'action research' which is needed — a qualitative study, where teachers are prepared to initiate, develop and monitor learning, to examine their own work and be prepared to share their experience with others.

Working parties provide a support structure, or point of contact, a source of encouragement and advice, and may be the most effective and cheapest form of in-service education, based on the self-help model. They offer a challenge to experiment, while at the same time they provide the security of developing a working relationship with colleagues who are familiar with the same experience and problems as oneself. The Project team is carrying out a study of the effectiveness of a selected group of working parties. When the results are available in 1982 they will provide a practical insight into this form of development whose aim is permanently to affect the school curriculum through encouraging local initiative.

The Schools Council policy is now to develop this model for curriculum development. The intention is that, with an initial stimulus and support from a central focus, the groups will be self-directive and self-generative. An enormous amount can be done using existing resources, but establishing new working relationships.

Phase Two of the Project has been concerned with creating, and understanding the role of, working parties. The conviction now exists that when Schools Council funding ends in August 1982 the working parties will continue to exist and carry on the work of the Project. If this happens, *Art and the Built Environment* will join that rather select band of curriculum development schemes that really have established themselves in schools.

Appendix: an evaluation of the project

Very little 'quantitative' evaluation has taken place within the art curriculum – for obvious reasons. It is not easy to measure developments in affective, expressive work. The study undertaken by Keith Gretton for *Art and the Built Environment* was therefore experimental, breaking new ground in attempting to analyse changes in students' critical awareness and aesthetic sensitivity.

The sample was small, but the results sufficiently encouraging to indicate that it is possible for an art curriculum to affect the attitudes and perceptions of students, and to demonstrate that this has in fact happened.

The extracts from his work which follow should therefore be read in the context of an innovatory attempt to assess the outcome of teaching activity which was itself new and investigatory. The full text of the Report is available separately from the Schools Council.

There were four aspects to the evaluation. The first, to assess the awareness of pupils as to key concepts in the built environment, was a questionnaire. The second, to assess pupils' ability in critical appraisal, relied on structured interview techniques. The third, based on the evaluator's wide experience in art education, was a review of the study methods and their effectiveness based on direct observation. The fourth was a discussion of the significance of the Project in the general setting of art education.

The Questionnaire

Art orientated environmental studies involve the study of the fact and the experience of the man-created world. Effort is made to develop understanding of colour, space, form, usage, materials, styles, and the totality of these messages imparted to the sensitised observer/participator. This approach to the subject naturally includes heritage studies as one factor in understanding the built environment.

In order to examine student understanding it is necessary to produce a breakdown of the subject discipline ('understanding' whilst not a stated aim of the Project does form a necessary basis for the development of feeling and critical response to the built environment). For the questionnaire the structuring of the discipline was approached in ways parallel to that used by advocates of 'Basic Design' in looking at art. As yet unpublished research, begun in 1974, was also used to construct the questionnaire. The form of the questionnaire was based on a checklist of 21 elements of architectural and environmental understanding. These were sorted in two alternative ways: one the product of teaching attitudes, the other related to the specialised professions that to a greater or lesser extent control the physical fact of our environment.

Structure One divided the two basic approaches to teaching into:
1 Townscape/Landscape *(Art and the Built Environment)*
   and
2 Buildings as Objects (Heritage Studies)

Structure Two was an arrangement of the checklist under four headings:
a The Substance of Buildings
b Planning and Urban Organization
c Historic Style and Period
d The Internal and/or External Environment

Checklist

Structure One: Townscape and Landscape ** Structure Two**

1	Scale in relation to man	abd
2	Scale between the parts (relating to a scale norm)	bc
3	The materials and form of townscape in relation to the colour and texture of the surrounding landscape	ab
4	Patterns of conservation and dereliction	bd
5	Social patterns seen through signs	bd
6	Patterns of land use; industrial, commercial, recreational and residential	bd
7	Visual pathways and the grammar of space	bd
8	Signs and symbols	b
9	Transport systems	·bc
10	Groundscape (texture, gradient, etc.)	bd

Structure One: Buildings as objects

11	Structural patterns	ac
12	Structure as social and symbolic messages	ac
13	Structure in relation to services	ab
14	Historic style and vernacular	ac
15	The significance of scale	ab
16	Mass, surface and plane	ad
17	Use of materials	ab
18	Hand, mass and reproduction	ac
19	Decoration and personalization	acd
20	Lifestyle and fashion	ac
21	Circulation	ad

The arrangement of the checklist was then used to devise questions which would, ideally, elicit responses from all students. A combination of specially photographed 35mm slides, duplicated drawings, plans and elevations were presented to student groups who were asked scripted questions related to each of the 21 elements of understanding. Because many of the questions asked students to list reactions, details or reasons, no time limit was imposed although the time variation between centres was under 10 per cent.

Interviews

In order to examine the extent of student involvement and their competence in critical appraisal it was necessary to rely on interviews with individuals and both small and large groups. While the questionnaire sought to elicit information on the type and extent of knowledge thought to be relevant to the Project, the interviews attempted to ascertain their ability to structure, present, support and develop critical perspectives.

The interviews took place at a wide variety of venues: in doorways, sheltering from the rain, in student common rooms over coffee, in studios while work was in progress and during presentations of work. As far as possible every attempt was made to make use of these informal situations to elicit 'real' responses from students.

In conducting the interviews, questions and answers were guided towards a predetermined set of criteria, which related to a student's development of critical skills and self-awareness as expressed in terms of objective and value judgements.

The chosen criteria can best be described as an expression of what might be called the ideal dimensions of critical awareness, for as in any rational view of criticism it must be recognized as personal, prejudiced and normally guilty of ignoring one of the dimensions included in the following list:

a   Willingness to adopt a critical position
b   Willingness to support a critical view with relevant documentation
c   Ability to recognize alternative readings of the problem
d   Ability to relate personal conviction to a particular reading of the problem
e   Ability to reassess a critical position and if necessary change position
f   Concern for the use of the most suitable techniques with which to communicate and support argument.

It was this list which formed the basic criteria adopted in looking at the profile of student involvement in relation to curriculum innovation and the particular study methods adopted during the progress of the Project.

Study Methods

'Steeple Chasing' (see pages 49-51) presented a simple and practical approach to what Gordon Cullen called 'serial vision'. By substituting a church steeple for Mount Fuji in Hokusai's print 'The Thirty-Six Views of Mount Fuji', students were able to make visual and historical reports on prescribed areas.

Townscape notation

As previously stated, a great deal of discussion was centred on attempting to explain the nature of *Art and the Built Environment* and how it differed fundamentally from simply using the environment as source material. In retrospect, 'townscape notation' can be seen as an important factor in focusing on study methods for critical appraisal.

'Townscape notation' used symbols and codes to record information, including signs to represent the quality of spatial experience. The system contained the three factors vital to any introduction to a subject; it was simple to understand and use, thus enabling all students to succeed; it reorientated normal patterns of perception; and it provided a basic introduction to the subject matter and aims of the Project in the form of simple instructions.

As a system it continues to prove successful with 9-15 year olds and with higher education students. Within the Project, however, it generally failed because of a self-consciousness resulting from the 'official' nature of a Schools Council Project in which a heightened sensitivity to questions of validity, suitability and correctness of subject ideology, at times outweighed the excitement of active curriculum exploration.

For many art teachers, both within and outside the Project, 'townscape notation' appeared as a radical shift away from the 'correct' practice of art education. Such a view is however mistaken as it regards 'townscape notation' as the educative experience rather than seeing the system as a tool to assist and gently force students to catalogue and order their experiences and make conscious critical assessments.

Townscape and building assessments, and sensory awareness

One of the main purposes of this evaluation is to isolate, define and illuminate the chief features of this complex Project. By dealing with both 'townscape assessment' and 'sensory awareness' in the same section it is intended to demonstrate that they are no more than different sides of the same coin, interrelated and interdependent. The two approaches attempt to deal with the same Project aim: how to tackle the vexing problem of critical and aesthetic awareness. As a study method, 'townscape assessment' represents the cool, intellectual and rational probe, while 'sensory awareness' proposes an emotional and meditative experience, open to the five senses – the classical versus the romantic; cerebral activity versus emotional response: Mondrian versus Van Gogh?

'Building impact' score sheets and 'word assessment' sheets or 'sensory walks' are all designed for recording perceptions and reporting feelings, but rely heavily on their positive use by teachers.

With one group of general studies students the 'sensory walk' produced a wide variety of responses. Two students recreated the sounds of Hatfield New Town on a multi-track tape. Another small group produced a game of town hazards. Others, perhaps more conventionally, graphically illustrated their experiences. What was most impressive about this group was their verbal animation, because the 'sensory walk' (like 'townscape assessment' for another group) had guided their perceptions of the environment in the *what* and the *how* of looking.

The only times when failure seemed to occur with the use of either study method was when too little maturation or gestation time was allowed between experience and work presentation.

As with all other subject specialists, art teachers are limited by the conventions of their subject. This is most evident in the assessment of art work where judgements are made by comparative methods relating work to one or other of the acceptable modes, styles and conventions of art modified by such considerations as vigour of execution (seen as personal conviction and emotional involvement) or delicacy and care in execution (seen as evidence of thoughtfulness and dedication). Faced with a section of townscape where conventional architectural (or tourist) responses are not applicable the tendency is to look for visual interest such as decorative brickwork, a door as a patch of colour, fancy ironwork, ridge tiles and roofscapes. This tendency can be termed the 'good sketch book approach'. 'Sensory awareness' and 'townscape assessments' represent successful attempts to avoid both heritage studies (a little history, geography and some tasteful lettering) and typical sketch book studies by concentrating on the quality of experience using all the senses, and thus are central to the methodology of *Art and the Built Environment*.

'The Appraisal of Buildings'

The third *Art and the Built Environment* edition of BEE presented an examination of a study method centred on looking at buildings within an environment rather than a general approach.

In the introduction to 'The Appraisal of Buildings', its major intention was stated, — namely, to propose an

157

alternative to the use of style as a major analytical factor in architectural criticism.

'The Appraisal of Buildings' as a scheme was based on the normal process of being aware of a building — we approach it seeing its 'context'; when close we recognize the ways in, the 'routes' we must take to enter it; closer still, we recognise the 'interface' between internal and private, and external and public, space; and finally, from the inside and outside, we recognise the 'grouping' of the parts that constitute the whole building. Context, routes, interface and grouping (CRIG) were to be used as the basis for critical appraisal of buildings. Because, as an approach, it provided a simple study method, it assisted tutors and students in the difficult task of establishing critical processes that go beyond mere like and dislike and, at the same time, avoided elitist and academic criticism based on the morphology of style.

In the Project centres it proved to be a highly successful introduction to criticism, but, because of its own internal text, it tended to result in bias towards social and planning studies with less consideration for the aesthetic needs of a community and little appreciation of the aesthetic qualities of an environment. However, more typical of the success of the scheme was this short piece written by a sixth form general studies student:

'This building has a character and mass closely related to the landscape. It has been well designed and details such as the roof tiles used decoratively giving the building a strong almost traditional yet modern look. The wall around the building is strong and dominant enclosing the private space around the building which is itself inviting and intimate.

The projections and indentations in the facade give a varied rhythm closely related to the pattern of the whole building.

At present the newness and solitary isolation of the building gives the impression of being somewhat out of place but when it matures and the surrounding houses and shops are built it will be seen as a natural part of the hillside as are the trees carefully left by the builders and planners.'

The Project and art education

In this evaluation the question which has, until now, been carefully and deliberately avoided is — to what extent is the making of art necessary or even desirable in attempting to accomplish the aims of the Project? The general standard of the art work produced by general studies and art students was high and the level of visual inventiveness, together with personal involvement in the production of those artifacts, indisputable. The interest and often excited enthusiasm of the tutors in the subject communicated itself to the students to such an extent that the work of general studies students was generally indistinguishable from that of A-level Art groups.

The level of discussion in the various centres seemed to be closely related to the observed skill of the tutors in asking searching questions, suggesting possible criteria and posing polemics to individuals and student groups. In the course of a long seminar more than 20 students in the 13-18 age range (all of whom had been or were involved with *Art and the Built Environment*) were asked to discuss

their project sites. The questioning led them through a majority of the 21 checklist architectural and environmental understandings. Many of the students who were involved with their second annual project demonstrated a remarkably high level of knowledge and understanding.

The two activities which engaged students for the major part of the time in almost all centres were the production of graphics (i.e. drawing, painting and photography) and discussion. As the proportion of time spent writing and preparing reports or scripts for slide shows was small, written work which ventured beyond the labelling of exhibits was not greatly in evidence. The reasons for this are probably twofold. Firstly, the only previously published and therefore accessible project was *'Front Door'* (Pimlico School), and secondly an unspoken and general desire on the part of tutors to education through the media of art. 'Front Door News', the Pimlico project broadsheet, was highly influential in the initial stages of the Project when tutors were most concerned about the *what* and *how* of study methods. As the Project progressed and tutors gained confidence in the involvement and guidance of students in this most daunting of topics, the number of written critiques increased.

In the development of critical skills, no matter how these are to be communicated, student progress is most effective when a basic pattern of investigation is introduced. In one centre this was simply stated as:
1 spend a long time looking at the subject all over, from various vantage points, in general and in detail;
2 name the subject (building), its present and past function; name the parts, the details, the location, its relationship, physical and functional, to the environment and other buildings;
3 establish criteria (and possible alternatives);
4 evaluate against criteria other than 'I like' and 'I dislike'.

The resultant studies, though small in number, were interesting in that the pattern of study involved students in a rigour which went beyond personal predilection and prejudice.

Art and the Built Environment has fashionable appeal corresponding closely with the general concern of the public and media about environmental topics. The belief of those connected with the Project is that a better visually educated public will be more rationally concerned and involved with the quality of urban surroundings. The possible longer lasting and more generally applicable effect of the Project on art education, rather than its subject matter, could be its attempt to encourage the development of critical studies freed from the constraints of historical studies. In the investigation and promotion of study of its chosen subject the Project has been highly successful, but to be aware of its success one would have had to have done the course or have been otherwise involved, for it is an area of activity which in any report on *Art and the Built Environment* will remain hidden behind the attractive facade of buildings painted, modelled, photographed and otherwise illustrated. For the students who participated, when the Project is a memory and when for most painting and drawing is, at best, a Sunday pastime, it is to be hoped that the experience of visual appraisal and critical evaluation will remain as the affective aspect of their visual education.

References

Chapter 1

1 *People and Planning* Report of the Committee on Public Participation in Planning
London, HMSO, 1969
2 Colin Ward and Anthony Fyson *Streetwork: The Exploding School*
London, Routledge and Kegan Paul, 1973

Chapter 3

1 Statement agreed by the International Working Meeting on Environmental Education in the School Curriculum, Nevada, 1970
2 Douglas McGregor Address to the Annual General Meeting of the Council for Environmental Education, 1973
Peter Berry *Environmental Education: A Survey of Schools*
London, Conservation Society, 1974
George Martin and Keith Wheeler (eds) *Insights into Environmental Education*
Edinburgh, Oliver and Boyd, 1976
Royal College of Art *Design in General Education, Parts 1 to 3*
London, Royal College of Art, 1976
Peter Green *Design Education: problem solving and visual experience*
London, Batsford, 1974
National Association for Design Education *Policy Statement*
Leicester, National Association for Design Education, 1974
Environmental Board *Final Report of the Working Party on Environmental Education*
London, DOE, 1978

Chapter 4

1 Brian Allison, Lecture given at Rolle College *Journal of the National Society for Art Education,* October 1978
2 Her Majesty's Inspectorate *Curriculum 11 to 16*
London, DES, 1977
3 Robert Witkin *The Intelligence of Feeling*
London, Heinemann, 1975
4 Op cit, Martin and Wheeler, 1976
5 Herbert Read *Education Through Art*
London, Faber and Faber, 1943
6 Op cit, Witkin, 1975
7 Malcolm Ross *The Creative Arts*
London, Heinemann, 1979
8 Rudolf Arnheim
9 Lance Wright *The Architectural Review* December 1976
10 Edmond Holmes *What Is and What Might Be*
London, 1911
11 Department of Education and Science *Art in Schools* Education Survey 11
London, HMSO, 1971

Chapter 5

1 Open University *Art and Environment* (TAD 292)
Course material
Milton Keynes, Open University
2 Eric Midwinter *Projections: An Educational Priority Area at Work*
London, Ward Lock, 1972
3 Wilfred Burns Seminar of the Artist Placement Group, Royal College of Art, December 1977
4 G Moore *Elements of a Genetic-structural Theory of the Development of Environmental Cognition* in EDRA 3
Los Angeles, UCLA, 1972
5 C Norberg-Schulz *Existence, Space and Architecture*
London, Studio Vista, 1971
6 C Norberg-Schulz *Meaning in Western Architecture*
London, Studio Vista, 1976

Chapter 16

1 Maurice Barrett *Art Education: A Strategy for Course Design*
London, Heinemann, 1979
2 Malcolm Ross *Arts and the Adolescent* Schools Council Working Paper no 54
London, Evans/Methuen Educational, 1975
3 Op cit, Her Majesty's Inspectorate, 1977

Bibliography

The literature potentially relevant to art and the built environment is enormous.
Our own brief list of basic books which teachers may find helpful is as follows:

GORDON CULLEN   *The Concise Townscape* Architectural Press
S E RASMUSSEN   *Experiencing Architecture* Chapman & Hall
YI-FU TUAN   *Topophilia* Prentice–Hall
IVOR DE WOLFE   *The Italian Townscape* Architectural Press
JOHN PRIZEMAN   *Your House, The Outside View* Hutchinson
ARTHUR KUTCHER   *Looking at London* Thames & Hudson
JOHN BERGER   *Ways of Seeing* Penguin
COLIN WARD & ANTHONY FYSON   *Streetwork: The Exploding School* Routledge & Kegan Paul
KEN BAYNES   *About Design* Design Council
ROBERT WITKIN   *The Intelligence of Feeling* Heinemann Educational Books
MALCOLM ROSS   *The Creative Arts* Heinemann Educational Books
NEIL POSTMAN & CHARLES WEINGARTNER   *Teaching as a Subversive Activity* Penguin
COLIN WARD   *The Child in the City* Architectural Press
MAURICE BARRETT   *Art Education: A Strategy for Course Design* Heinemann Educational Books